NORFOLK

GRAND

LUDLOW

ESSEX

BETH
HAME
HAGA

DAVID SILVER'S
HARDWARE STORE

GELLIS'S
KOSHER
SAUSAGE
FACTORY

ISAAC GELLIS
EST. 1873
ovisions
LE · RETAIL
· OFFICE

KALMEN
LONDON'S
MATZO
FACTORY

FORWARD

SEWARD
PARK

NATHAN
HUTKOFF'S
HOME

FORWARD
BUILDING

JEFFERSON

EDUCATIONAL
ALLIANCE

CLINTON

RUTGERS

GARDEN
CAFETERIA

HEBREW
SHELTERING
SOCIETY

MADISON

N

LANDMARK OF THE SPIRIT

LANDMARK OF THE SPIRIT

The Eldridge Street Synagogue

ANNIE POLLAND

FOREWORD BY BILL MOYERS

YALE UNIVERSITY PRESS   NEW HAVEN AND LONDON

Published with the assistance of the Institute for Israel and Jewish Studies, Columbia University.

Designed by Gregg Chase.
Set in Fournier MT type by Tseng Information Systems, Inc.
Printed in Canada by Friesens.

Library of Congress Cataloging-in-Publication Data
Polland, Annie, 1973–
Landmark of the spirit : the Eldridge Street Synagogue / Annie Polland.
p. cm.
Includes bibliographical references and index.
ISBN 978-0-300-12470-5 (alk. paper)
1. Eldridge Street Synagogue (New York, N.Y.). 2. Synagogues—New York (State)—New York—History.
3. Jews—New York (State)—New York—History. 4. Judaism—New York (State)—New York—History. I. Title.
BM225.N442E437 2009
296.09747'1—dc22
2008022106

A catalogue record for this book is available from the British Library.

This paper meets the requirements of ANSI/NISO Z39.48-1992 (Permanence of Paper).
It contains 30 percent postconsumer waste (PCW) and is certified by the Forest Stewardship Council (FSC).

10 9 8 7 6 5 4 3 2 1

*For my grandmother Inez Schoenfeld and
in memory of my grandfather Harry Schoenfeld*

Contents

Foreword

Go to the eldridge street synagogue and you will see that Thomas Carlyle was right when he said, "The past is a world, and not a void of gray haze."

Flesh and blood, soul and bone were those men and women who built that house of worship. They pressed into its quarters in such numbers that at times a guard had to be stationed at the entrance to manage the crowd. "Lawyers, merchants, artisans, clerks, peddlers and laborers," families, friends, visitors, and strangers gathered to hear the voice of the Lord God above the din of the tenements and the streets and the alleyways. Jehovah had competition.

This was more than a house of worship. This was the portal of a new life in a new land for the largest wave of immigrants ever. They had found a home in a far country, and this synagogue was where they held family reunions. There was news to be shared from the old country, tips on surviving in America, gossip about erring brothers and sisters, rumors of broken deals and broken hearts. They would, the records show, announce with joy the betrothals and births, the new beginnings. They would receive with sadness word of the loss of friend or kin. Tales would be told as well, of fortunes found and lost by the brave and foolhardy among them who had moved ever westward in the restless search for manna, to distant places with strange names: Cleveland, Saint Louis, Chicago. One-third of all eastern European Jews were transplanted to the United States during the last half of the nineteenth century, and the Eldridge Street Synagogue—the first they built in this new world—became a crossroads of their hopes and aspirations.

Do stones speak? Go there and listen. You will hear, I swear, the endless murmur of ten thousand tongues expressing wonder at being alive, wonder at being in New York City, and wonder at being free. You and I are so free today that it is almost impossible to understand the exultation they must have felt in walking along Eldridge Street without the boots of the Cossack tromping behind. They had never before lived in a country where freedom of religion existed. Let me say it again: They had never before lived in a country where freedom of religion existed. Even here in New Amsterdam in the beginning, two centuries earlier, they would have been trespassers. Governor Peter Stuyvesant had complained to the Dutch West India Company—the owners of the colony—that Jews must not be granted "free and public exercise of their abominable religion," because "giving them liberty we cannot refuse the Lutherans and Catholics."

My own spiritual forebears tasted the same bitter fruit. They were Baptists, hounded from Europe for being different, but here in the New World they found an established religion whose authority was suffocating. They were flogged for teaching "damnable errors." They were fined and imprisoned for worshipping without permission. They were harassed for refusing to pay taxes to support ministers of the state religion. One of them, Roger Williams, was expelled from Massachusetts for being a nonconformist and spent a long hard season in the wilderness. He emerged to found Providence, Rhode Island, as a settlement whose cornerstone was absolute religious liberty for all—Jew and Turk included, said Williams. He secured a royal charter, the first of its kind in the world, positing that "no person within the said colony, at any time hereafter shall be any wise molested, punished, disquieted, or called to question, for any differences of opinion in matters of religion," and the idea took hold.

Standing on Eldridge Street, I could imagine Roger Williams spiritually at home there, pleased at the flowering of the religious liberty for which he and others had toiled. In the last half of the nineteenth century the fertile soil of liberty was producing in America a veritable thicket of religions, so when the Jews of eastern Europe arrived, they found a place freely to be Jewish. No more hiding behind drawn shutters to worship. No more makeshift temples in the basements of stores. No more asking anyone's permission.

Here they could go public, and they did. They published in brick and mortar: go to the synagogue and read. You will not find anywhere a more eloquent expression of Jewish faith and American freedom.

That the Eldridge Street Synagogue has stood more than a hundred years is a miracle. Through the twentieth century, as synagogues all over "civilized Europe" were being profaned and demolished, this one proclaimed a message as old as the story of Moses—the Faith of the Fathers—and as bold as the Declaration that in this new order of the ages, here in the United States, all of us are created equal.

Just consider the architecture. Our nation's founding fathers were intrigued by the numeric rhythms of this ancient faith, so I can imagine one of our first gifted architects, Thomas Jefferson (if he had lived but another three score and ten years), relishing the courageous symbolism of the synagogue's facade—the two tablets of the Ten Commandments; the three points of the central pediments for the three fathers of Israel, Abraham, Isaac, and Jacob; the four doors for the four mothers, Sarah, Rebecca, Leah, and Rachel; the cluster of five small windows for the five books of Moses; and the twelve roundels of the magnificent rose window for the twelve tribes of Israel.

Surely, too, would James Madison have smiled if he could have stood there, just a few blocks from where George Washington took the oath of office as president, and seen a house of refuge built in this new nation by people who had been scourged, besieged, hounded, and persecuted on account of conscience in the old nations of Europe. Between the writing of the Constitution in the 1780s and the raising of this synagogue in the 1880s runs a genealogy of freedom. We Americans in the early twenty-first century are its heirs, descendants, and stewards.

It is no mere building that is the focus of this book. The Eldridge Street Synagogue is a magnificent building, to be sure, and should be treasured and admired for beauty's sake. New York City is enriched by every particular of its glorious ornamentation and grandeur—from the carved balustrade around the cantor's platform to the four corners of the bimah, with its brass torchères and glass shades; from the graceful hemispherical domes over the balcony to the round-arched windows; from the gold stars on the blue vaulted ceiling to the walnut ark on the east wall, facing Jerusalem.

But this synagogue is a landmark of the spirit as well: the spirit of an ancient people on a new exodus and the spirit of a new nation committed to the old idea of liberty. Every synagogue is a means of keeping Jewish consciousness alive, but this one's mission of memory is unique in the world. Four-fifths of today's American Jews descend from the eastern European refugees who came in that exodus. The Eldridge Street Synagogue connects the generations one to another. It is also sacred ground to many of us who are *not* Jewish: it is sacred to the very love of freedom that drew *all* our forebears here.

So what is our obligation? A wise man of the Jewish faith once said, "In remembrance is the secret of redemption." I puzzled over that a long time, until I read again George Orwell's *1984*. In that novel, you will remember, Big Brother banishes history to the memory hold, where inconvenient facts disappear. The power of despotism, as Orwell describes it, rests not alone on the police but also on a complete rejection of the past — its rejection and abolition. The past, you see, is indispensable to freedom. Consciousness is memory. People without it are prisoners of the present, ruled by those who can say that what was so, is no longer so. In accepting the Nobel Prize for Literature, Czeslaw Milosz, a Polish émigré now teaching in this country, said: "We are surrounded today by fictions about the past. . . . The number of books in various languages which deny that the Holocaust ever took place, that it was invented by Jewish propaganda, has exceeded one hundred. If such an insanity is possible, is a complete loss of memory as a permanent state of mind improbable?" Such a loss of memory may be willful. "Our planet gets smaller every year, with its fantastic proliferation of mass media, and is witnessing a process that escapes definition, characterized by a refusal to remember."

A refusal to remember. Abraham Lincoln would have been appalled. He knew the power of memory to shape the continuity and character of a people. In his first inaugural address, Lincoln talked about the "mystic chords of memory, stretching from every battlefield and every patriot grave to every living heart and hearthstone all over this broad land." These words define something especially human, a power of transmitting experience from one generation to another, down through the corridors of time. Words, experiences, connect us emotionally and spiritually to the human beings who came before and who will follow.

Do stones speak? They do on Eldridge Street. And through the words of Annie Polland's beautiful and important book. Hear them: "In remembrance is the secret of redemption."

Bill Moyers

Acknowledgments

THIS BOOK IS DEDICATED to my grandparents Inez and Harry Schoenfeld, two Milwaukeeans who never made it to the Eldridge Street Synagogue but whose stories of their immigrant parents, devotion to their religion, and love for their grandchildren led me to explore Jewish history.

This book helps bring the history of the Eldridge Street Synagogue beyond Eldridge Street, and it is able to do so in large part owing to the photographs and other images. Michael Weinstein, Chairman of the Board of Directors of the Museum at Eldridge Street, made it possible for this book to be published in this beautiful form, and I deeply appreciate his generosity and also the instrumental role he played in helping to galvanize support for the extraordinary restoration. This book is also published with the assistance of a grant from the Institute for Israel and Jewish Studies at Columbia University, for which I am grateful.

Telling the story of the Eldridge Street Synagogue put me in debt to many people. I am indebted to the docents I met when I joined the staff of the Eldridge Street Project, now the Museum at Eldridge Street. Their devotion to the building was as stalwart as the congregation's, and they appeared weekly to educate the public about its history. Even before proper heating was installed, they came in their boots and layers of clothing and served as "pullers-in" — standing at the door and ushering in passersby. I would like to thank George Beckwith, Roberta Berken, Beulah Buchwald (z'l), Edward Cheng, Clarice Feinman, Barry Feldman, Naomi Gat, Alan Ginsberg, Lyla Glener, Anita Graber, Julius Graber (z'l), John

Heller, Jane Herman, Gisa Indenbaum, Linda Katz, and Pamela Rytsis. I would also like to thank the dozens of docents who have joined the team in the past few years, whose energetic curiosity about both the synagogue's history and today's visitors enliven the building.

The staff of the Museum at Eldridge Street have been a constant source of support and encouragement. It is an honor to work alongside Victoria Baritz, Eva Brune, Phyllis Freed, Hanna Griff, Xiao Situ, and Amy Waterman. Bonnie Dimun, Executive Director, with her generosity and resolve, and Amy Stein Milford, Deputy Director, with her creativity and friendship, were a great source of inspiration.

The founders of the Eldridge Street Project, Roberta Brandes Gratz and William Josephson, and the board of directors not only were committed to the physical restoration of the building but also generated and nurtured the vision of the synagogue as a cultural and educational center. I thank Susan B. Boshwit, Mildred Caplow, Lorinda Ash Ezersky, Ester Fuchs, Roberta Brandes Gratz, Alyssa Greenberg, R. Jeffrey Gural, Armand Lindenbaum, Jonathan L. Mechanic, Mark Mirsky, David Moore, Richard Rabinowitz, Joseph B. Rosenblatt, P. Sheridan Schechner, Orna Shulman, David Sitzer, Kenneth L. Stein, Steven Walsey, Michael Weinstein, Jeffrey Wilks, and Howard Zar.

The documents, oral histories, and research that were gathered over the years served as the building blocks for this book. Dr. Richard Rabinowitz, Dr. Amy Waterman, and Minda Novek's collection of court documents, mergers, and deeds and their commentary, "Historical Detective Work," were indispensable in piecing together the early years of the congregation. Fruma Mohrer's and Daniel Soyer's translations of sections of the Eldridge Street Minutes helped immeasurably. Renee Newman, Maria Schlanger, and Amy Waterman's National Historic Landmark report and Dr. Celia Bergoffen's report on the *mikvah* were indispensable sources. Crucial to the understanding of the Eldridge Street Synagogue's history and its place in American Judaism was the work conducted by Dr. Jeffrey Gurock. The oral histories with former congregants conducted in the 1980s and 1990s by the Eldridge Street Project board members, staff, and volunteers Marni Davis, Beth Edberg, Roberta Brandes Gratz, Renee Newman, Judy Tenney, and Suzanne Wasserman were another valuable source. I was especially grateful to meet several former congregants, Naomi Groob Fuchs, Edwin Margolius, and Max Smith, and I savor the conversations I had, and continue to have, with them. The late Judge Paul P. E. Bookson's vision for the congregation and Tova Bookson's leadership of the congregation today keep the immigrant founders' traditions alive.

I am profoundly grateful to the talented team of photographers and artists at Eldridge Street. The photographs by Edward Cheng, Kate Milford, and Rachel Rabhan and the watercolor map by Adrienne Ottenberg (which decorates the endpapers of this book) make the beauty of the synagogue and the neighborhood accessible to those far beyond the Lower East Side. All illustrations reproduced in this book are from the Collection of the Museum at Eldridge Street unless otherwise indicated.

I would like to thank Nina Cohen, Rebecca Kobrin, and Tony Michels, who read early drafts of this book, as well as the reviewers who read the manuscript for Yale University Press, for their helpful comments.

Ileene Smith shepherded this project along, and I am truly grateful. Thanks are also due to Ileene's husband, Howard Sobel, and their daughter, Becca Sobel, whose enthusiastic review of an Eldridge Street Synagogue tour was the catalyst for this book. Mary Pasti's excellent edits and good cheer made the final months of my work on this project a delight.

My parents, Linda and Jeff Rosen, and my parents-in-law, Joan and George Smrtic, provided much-needed encouragement, while Sara Polland and Sam Polland provided much-needed humor.

Michael Smrtic contributed the most to this project. His thorough editing of every draft was the process through which I found and sharpened my arguments. His endless knowledge of and love for the humanities and his incomparable wit and charm make him not only a brilliant husband but also now a wonderful teacher for our daughter. Lily considers the Eldridge Street Synagogue to be a second home, and I hope that as she grows she will learn more about the stories it has to tell about American Jewish history.

LANDMARK OF THE SPIRIT

ONE

A Landmark Synagogue

THE WESTERN SIDE OF Eldridge Street is home to a dizzying array of activities. Workers unload vegetable crates, merchants buy restaurant supplies, residents and tourists visit Chinese bakeries and noodle shops, and Buddhist priests offer sidewalk feasts to the gods. So vibrant is the mix of commerce, social activity, and religion that movie and television crews in search of a New York Chinatown scene often set up their cameras here to capture it on film. But their shots tend to omit the eastern side of the street, for there, in the center of the block, stands a synagogue. Its cream-colored brick, its Moorish finials, and its Star of David ornamentation catch the eye. What is a synagogue doing in the heart of Chinatown?

When it opened in September 1887, in what was the heart of the Jewish Lower East Side, the Eldridge Street Synagogue surprised spectators then, too. New York's east European Jewish population, made up of peddlers and tailors and their families, had worshipped in small, nondescript storefronts, partitioned tenement halls, and churches converted into synagogues. Although they eventually built dozens of synagogues, as well as notable, even palatial secular spaces—banks, newspaper headquarters, and theaters—in 1887 nothing in the neighborhood's architecture announced the Jewish presence as strikingly as the Eldridge Street Synagogue did. Opening just in time for the Jewish High Holidays, the synagogue permanently altered the streetscape and skyline of the Lower East Side, attracting not only downtown and uptown Jews but also reporters from New York

West Side of Eldridge Street
   For forty years, Eldridge Street was part of the Jewish Lower East Side. Today it is part of a dynamic and
expanding Chinatown. Photograph by Edward Cheng.

City's leading papers, one of whom heralded the "elegant" and "magnificent"
synagogue as "one of the finest Hebrew places of worship in the city."[1]

   For the tens of thousands of Jewish immigrants already settled on the Lower
East Side, as for the hundreds of thousands who would arrive in the coming decades, New York's first great east European synagogue expressed the hope that
the immigrants' religion and culture would flourish on American soil.[2] For forty
years after the synagogue's dedication, it was sustained by "lawyers, merchants,
artisans, clerks, peddlers and laborers" who gathered to celebrate holidays, mark
life-cycle events, and debate communal issues.[3] Cantorial concerts and Sabbath
sermons drew crowds; daily study sessions attracted a core constituency. When
longtime members moved uptown at the turn of the twentieth century, new immigrants replenished the congregation. But by the 1920s the population, as economi-
cally and geographically mobile as earlier immigrants, had dispersed far beyond
the Lower East Side, and immigration quotas stemmed the tide of arrivals. Still,

the members who remained, many of whom operated small neighborhood businesses, kept the congregation going. By the 1950s a depleted but stalwart congregation could no longer afford the repairs needed to maintain the building, or even to heat its sanctuary, and met instead in the street-level chapel.

In the 1970s and 1980s the congregation still prayed in the street-level chapel, but the building itself was in grave disrepair, its cracked foundations, leaky roof, and unsound structure "held up only by strings to heaven." In 1971, New York University professor Gerard Wolfe persuaded Benjamin Markowitz, the sexton, to show him the sealed-off sanctuary. Although pigeons roosted in the balcony, grime covered the stained-glass windows and painted surfaces, and dust blanketed the wooden surfaces, Wolfe was amazed by its beauty, and together both Wolfe and Markowitz began to lead visitors on tours of the sanctuary. Hoping to preserve and ultimately restore the building, the journalist and preservationist Roberta Brandes Gratz and the attorney William Josephson incorporated the not-for-profit nonsectarian Eldridge Street Project (now renamed the Museum at Eldridge Street) in 1986, which mounted the largest independent restoration in New York City not supported by or attached to an institution or government agency. When raising funds and organizing the restoration fostered recognition of the site's potential as an educational and cultural space, the project sought and secured National Historic Landmark status and introduced tours and programs that brought tens of thousands of visitors to the synagogue.[4]

In 2007 the Eldridge Street Synagogue became once again the magnificent edifice that had greeted throngs of worshippers 120 years earlier. From Eldridge Street, visitors can survey the same cream facade that immigrants beheld on opening day; inside, they can marvel at the fifty-foot barrel-vaulted ceiling, the richly hued stained-glass windows, and the majestic carved-walnut ark, still lined with its original crimson velvet. This restored synagogue is one of the last remaining—and arguably the best-preserved—edifices built by the east European immigrants who made the Lower East Side the world's largest Jewish city around 1900. Its history is perpetuated today in two separate but complementary ways. On the Sabbath and holidays, congregation members, who have, across the generations, never missed a Sabbath service, worship in the Orthodox tradition of their grandparents and great-grandparents. On Sundays and weekdays, the Museum at

Eldridge Street explores the context of their worship, explaining to visitors of diverse ages and backgrounds how the immigrant founders and their children lived, worked, and prayed on the Lower East Side.

The museum's tours treat the synagogue as a historical artifact. Its architectural elements—the facade, reader's platform, even the lighting fixtures—prompt discourses on the shared history of the congregation and the Lower East Side. The architectural elements work well as prompts because the restorers, with meticulous sensitivity, retained elements and finishes that show the passage of time. The undulations left on the sanctuary's pine floors, formed by worshippers' feet rocking back and forth, are perhaps the most striking reminders of the past. A ring of light bulbs encircling the ark's Ten Commandments was added in 1907, when the congregation installed electricity to attract congregants as some established members moved uptown and new neighborhood synagogues drew others away. On the northern balcony wall, a section of plaster and lathwork interrupts the stenciling and shows where water damage stripped away layers of decorative paint, plaster, and wood during the half-century when both the congregation's membership and the Lower East Side's Jewish population declined. As beautiful as the building is, its real power lies in its ability to convey the history of the immigrants and the challenges they faced in adapting to a new land.[5]

The congregation, Kahal Adath Jeshurun, lay the synagogue's cornerstone in 1886 and celebrated its final mortgage payment in 1945. In retrospect, we can link the congregation's history to the growth and decline of the Lower East Side's Jewish population, but from the congregation's perspective on opening day, the synagogue was an experiment, and the course was debated every step of the way. Pioneer presidents, enterprising women congregants, star-quality cantors, and gifted orators grappled with the challenges of creating a viable Orthodox congregation in a city and country that both encouraged and threatened traditional customs. The story of the congregation's efforts to create and maintain a sacred space in what east European rabbis termed a *treyfene medine*, or impure land, becomes a case study of the opportunities and obstacles facing immigrant groups carving out a space—physical, mental, and spiritual—for religious life in America.[6]

East European Jewish immigrants came to America in search of economic opportunities and political and religious freedom. Throughout eastern Europe—

Chandelier
The chandelier in the sanctuary was originally lit by gas, but in 1907 the congregation voted to install electricity. The congregation kept the original Victorian brass fixture but turned the arms upside down to accommodate lightbulbs. Photograph © 2007 by Kate Milford.

Russia, Austria-Hungary, Romania — industrialization had brought extreme economic dislocation as struggling merchants and artisans found their production of services and goods far outpaced by Western output. The economic shift was compounded by overpopulation in Jewish communities, spurring migration to large cities throughout Europe and America. In Russia, outbreaks of pogroms in the aftermath of Tsar Alexander II's assassination in 1881 and the ensuing restrictions on Jewish educational, residential, and occupational options further encouraged Jews, especially the young, to seek a better life in America. Between 1880 and 1924, two and a half million east European Jews came to the United States. Close to 85 percent of them came to New York City, and approximately 75 percent of those settled initially on the Lower East Side, which by 1890 "bristled with Jews." There they found homes in tenements and work in the mushrooming garment factories and the pushcart-laden streets.[7]

Lightbulbs on the Ark
    The bare lightbulbs that form a ring around the Ten
Commandments on the ark announced to all visitors the
congregation's new technology—electricity—adopted in a
competition with nearby synagogues to increase membership.
Photograph © 2007 by Kate Milford.

Although, in theory, freedom of religion and separation of church and state
encouraged religious life in their new country, American law and culture provided
no formal support for rabbinical authority, which made religious officials reluc-
tant to emigrate to the United States and immigrants already there less inclined
to accept rabbinical authority. The United States, and New York City specifically,
presented immigrants with an astounding array of educational and occupational
options, which often challenged the practices of Orthodox Judaism. A six-day

Lathwork

This swath of wall was left unrestored to show the water damage in the mid-twentieth century that stripped the lathwork of much of its plaster and paint. Photograph © 2007 by Kate Milford.

workweek that included Saturday and, through blue laws, restricted Sunday commerce offered many immigrants little choice but to work on Saturday, the Jewish Sabbath. Retaining a steady and solvent membership where religious participation was voluntary, congregations were in competition, and traditional Sabbath observances posed an ongoing challenge transformed efforts to establish traditional Jewish congregations into experiments.[8]

The Eldridge Street congregation grew in part because its institutional roots extended back to 1852, providing its members with more than thirty years of experience in their adopted city. In 1886, President Sender Jarmulowsky headed a group of leaders who moved the congregation from a converted church on Allen Street into a brand-new synagogue. The idea for a synagogue had been translated into a reality in fewer than eighteen months, but the skills and contacts the synagogue leaders drew on to steer the process had been cultivated in their years as American bankers, plate-glass dealers, kosher sausage manufacturers, and real-

estate investors. The congregation held annual elections and crafted a "constitution," fitting the rules for worship, study, communal service, and synagogue
leadership into their new country's "bylaws," "articles," and "amendments." In
another nod to American social and economic trends, this congregation — which
limited its membership to Sabbath observers — had no qualms about selling special
High Holiday tickets to Lower East Side residents who were not synagogue members (and therefore most likely worked on the Sabbath). An acute understanding
of American economic, social, and cultural trends and a skillful integration of up-
to-date ideas into the management of the congregation produced a synagogue
that attracted Jews from all over eastern Europe, with a range of economic and
occupational statuses and religious sensibilities.

The primary goal of the Eldridge Street Synagogue's congregation was upholding Jewish law. Some worshippers came twice a day, some came weekly, and
others came once a year. The congregation hired rabbis to lead study sessions,
developed and maintained an impressive library of Jewish commentary, supported
permanent rabbis and rabbinical travel and studies, and sponsored neighborhood
yeshivas, or academies of Talmudic learning. Congregants and guests celebrated
Jewish holidays and organized weddings and bar mitzvahs. In times of mourning,
the congregation's *khevre kedishe,* or burial society, performed one of the most
valued of the Jewish commandments, preparing the deceased for burial, ensuring
that the deceased's family had enough people to meet prayer quorums, and offering comfort as the family mourned. Each year the congregation donated thousands of pounds of matzos, kosher meat, and wine to those in need of Passover
provisions, and each week the Ladies' Auxiliary sponsored meals for the homeless.
By depositing a coin in a six-slotted charity box, worshippers could link themselves to the broader Jewish community, for the donations supported Lower East
Side charitable institutions and settlements in Palestine.

Despite the many visible successes, the synagogue was the target of scathing
criticism from the start. Its beauty led some contemporary observers to bemoan
the amounts of money lavished on a physical structure in the absence of needed
educational services. The tremendous expense apportioned to secure a cantor,
albeit an extremely learned one, struck some as scandalous when compared to the
paltry incomes eked out by learned rabbis and scholars. In other corners, socialists

Constitution, 1913
Rather than call the book of rules by a Yiddish or Hebrew name,
the congregation adopted the terminology of their adopted country.

took the religious leaders to task for engaging in "business Judaism" and shirking the greater responsibility of addressing the problems besieging the Jewish immigrant workforce.[9]

At first glance, the contemporary critics may seem to have been right: the Eldridge Street Synagogue was neither a great center of formal learning nor an outright champion of the workers' struggle. The minutes of the congregation show that the leaders devoted more time and money to repairing chandeliers and painting ceilings than to establishing a Hebrew school. Contracts that explicitly forbade hired preachers from addressing political matters before the congregation suggest that the congregational leadership did not care to dive into the political, social, and economic currents swirling around the Lower East Side at the turn of the twentieth century.[10]

Whatever the leadership planned, the congregation—and the immigrant community of the Lower East Side as a whole—made use of the sanctuary not merely as a space for worship but also as a venue in which to support communal institutions and debate social issues. People came to Eldridge Street to pray, certainly, but also to learn about issues and tensions within the Jewish community with respect to Orthodox Judaism and, more broadly, immigrants' social and economic adaptation to New York City. The synagogue was a vital community center, not a refuge from America but a place where people could wrestle with the challenges that America posed, a place where religious and economic life intertwined. Efforts toward maintaining Orthodox Judaism at the turn of the twentieth century necessarily involved fundraising: money to form Jewish charitable associations, money to establish schools, money to build Jewish hospitals. This need was met by those who had adapted to, and succeeded in, the American business environment. Immigrants' religious adaptation also has to be understood in the context of an economic environment that more or less necessitated Saturday work. The Eldridge Street Synagogue's leaders sensed this relationship and accordingly supported the Sabbath Association, an organization that worked to repeal blue laws in Albany, and supported storekeepers who kept their shops closed on the Jewish Sabbath.[11]

This awareness of and effort to address the modern world's challenges to Orthodox Judaism spurred the Eldridge Street Synagogue's leaders to improve Orthodox Jewish life for its members and the Jewish community at large. They partnered with Beth Hamedrash Hagadol to spearhead a union of congregations, the Association of American Hebrew Orthodox Congregations, and sounded a call to action: "We find that our religion is neglected and our Law held in light esteem. . . . Is it not our duty to prevent our children and grandchildren from straying?" In early 1888 the association gathered at the Eldridge Street Synagogue to collect subscriptions for the effort to import Rabbi Jacob Joseph to New York.[12] Although this initial venture proved unsuccessful, the congregation engaged in numerous other attempts to solidify east European Orthodoxy in the United States, including the establishment of the successful Orthodox Union in 1898. The union convened at the synagogue, and several of the synagogue's leaders held office in it.

Even more significant than the press-worthy federation of rabbinical notables was the routine way congregational leaders integrated a concern for the broader community into their biweekly meetings. In 1900, for example, President Nathan Hutkoff proposed that the congregation take the lead in bringing Rabbi Jacob David Willowski, author of a forthcoming commentary on the Jerusalem Talmud, from Slutsk, in what is now Belarus, to New York: "The president takes up the matter, that several orthodox congregations would like the Rabbi of Slutsk with them for a few months. Perhaps his presence will contribute somewhat to an improvement in the state of Judaism. In the meantime, the congregation should contribute to his living expenses. Resolved, to give full authority to the president, Mr. Nathan Hutkoff, and to the vice president, Avrohom Yitschok Fein, and to Moshe Ziskind Feinsilber to participate in the committee and they are empowered to decide on contributions up to $5.00 a week. Also, it is resolved that the Shul [synagogue] should contribute another $100.00 in addition to the money that was pledged for the Slutsker Rabbi and to charge the money to the accounts of those who had made the pledges."

The congregation met democratically, considered Hutkoff's proposal, voted to pledge the $100.00, and also authorized its leaders to sit on a neighborhood council, attend its meetings, and donate additional funds to pay for the rabbi's expenses. The congregation itself would reap from this financial and time commitment only the hope that Rabbi Willowski's presence would "contribute somewhat to an improvement in the state of Judaism." Incidents like this reflect the seriousness with which the congregation regarded their religion. Even when their own finances were low or their energies tied up in keeping the synagogue's finances afloat and its building intact, they often paused to devote even more time and money in the hope of improving Orthodox Judaism in America.[13]

In addition to being engaged with Orthodoxy, the congregation kept a close watch on the immigrant community's social and economic struggles, repeatedly offering its greatest asset—its spacious sanctuary—to helping east European immigrants address welfare issues. Many of the Eldridge Street Synagogue's leaders were among those who founded the Hakhnoses Orkhim, or Hebrew Sheltering

Society, in 1889 to provide newly arrived immigrants with lodging and work. Besides allocating funds to this society (which would merge with the Hebrew Immigrant Aid Society in 1909 to form the Hebrew Sheltering and Immigrant Aid Society), the congregation held fundraisers in the sanctuary. A congregational meeting rarely passed without a visit from a neighboring institution—a hospital, orphanage, school, or other charity—asking for subscriptions and contributions, which were always granted. On social issues, the congregation demonstrated a sophisticated ability to separate matters of church and state, allowing people of diverse ideological and religious beliefs to occupy the podium. At a mass meeting in 1900, for example, eight hundred East Siders crowded into the synagogue to hear Dr. Felix Adler, a former Reform rabbi and founder of the Ethical Culture Society, lecture on fighting neighborhood crime. Adler had rejected Judaism to establish what he considered a more universal Ethical Culture, and admitted to the audience "that it was the first time in twenty-seven years that he had spoken in a synagogue."[14] Although the congregation would never have allowed Adler to lead a religious service or deliver a sermon, they understood that his involvement in progressive city issues made him especially qualified to speak about the pressing issue of crime on the Lower East Side.

Within the walls of the synagogue, immigrants forged an American Jewish identity that blended patriotism to their new country with a responsibility to Jews throughout the world, especially communities in eastern Europe. In 1889 the congregation decorated the synagogue in honor of the centennial of George Washington's inauguration and, in 1901, held a memorial service for President William McKinley. During World War I, the congregation commissioned and displayed an American flag with stars for each one of the congregation's sons serving in the war. In the aftermath of eastern European pogroms and during World War I, the congregation organized concerts and assemblies to raise money for afflicted Jewish communities overseas. Even though the direct beneficiaries of these fundraisers were the Jews in eastern Europe, the synagogue assemblies assuaged the immigrants' need to maintain a connection to their native communities even as they strove to Americanize.[15]

The three flagholders affixed to window sills to display American flags against the facade of the building exhibit the seamless blending of traditional

Flagholder on Windowsill

      This is one of three flagholders, each with a five-pointed
American star at its base, that remain attached to windowsills on the
synagogue's western wall. Three American flags used to hang over
the synagogue's facade, the cloth Stars and Stripes forming a link to
the terra-cotta Stars of David. In 1918 the congregation decided to
"hang out an American flag . . . with a star for each young man from
the synagogue in the army." Photograph © 2006 by Kate Milford.

Orthodox and patriotic American influences. The congregation itself, however,
was full of contentious debate over the best way to create a successful Orthodox congregation in America. The very size of the synagogue attracted a diverse
membership—some rich, some poor, and many in-between. Consequently, a diversity of opinions competed with regard to lay leadership, the role of the rabbi

and the cantor, children's education, and the movement of established members uptown. That the congregation's constitution repeatedly emphasized the need for "order" and "decorum" and instituted fines for those who talked during services or meetings and that the minutes record repeated outbreaks attests not only to the ongoing struggle to incorporate an American middle-class sense of decorum into the synagogue service but also to the feistiness of the congregants.[16]

The congregation weathered these debates and established an impressive reputation. The synagogue's persistence into the 1930s and the congregation's ability to fundraise to pay off the mortgage in the mid-1940s speak to the congregation's success in cultivating a unity and a sense of history among members and within the Jewish community. As Rabbi Israel "Idel" Idelson commented at the fiftieth-anniversary celebration of the synagogue: "We must remember those members who built the greatest and most beautiful synagogue." The longtime president David Parnes made the same point: "Thanks to the loyalty of many members and businessmen we have made it through all the crises." This was not just the rhetoric of an anniversary celebration; years later, the children of congregants repeatedly commented on their parents' abiding love for the synagogue.[17]

The immigrants who congregated at the Eldridge Street Synagogue were not simply seeking shelter in a sacred space in an otherwise impure land. Rather, they were taking what they had learned in the American environment and applying it to their religious center. They surely argued and disagreed and negotiated and split and synthesized, but they were devoted to the synagogue they had built, and its history is the story of how they became American Jews.

TWO

Laying the Cornerstone

O N SUNDAY MORNING, November 14, 1886, a "magnificent parade" gathered at a construction site encompassing the lots of 12-14-16 Eldridge Street. The organizers, members of Beth Hamedrash and Congregation Holkhe Yosher Vizaner, had merged with the express purpose of constructing a synagogue. Finally, after months of negotiations, lot purchases, and a name change, the day had come for the laying of the cornerstone. The men and women of the new, merged congregation, Kahal Adath Jeshurun, had spared no expense: they had sent invitations to "upstanding visitors," purchased new chairs, served refreshments, and decorated the site. Both local and uptown dignitaries delivered speeches. Rabbi Henry Pereira Mendes, representing the oldest congregation in the United States, Shearith Israel; Rabbi Yitskhok Margolies, from the downtown Pike Street Synagogue; and a politician, the coroner Ferdinand Levy, addressed the crowds. Sender Jarmulowsky, the congregation's president, thanked Nathan Hutkoff, the congregation's treasurer and head of the building committee, who had donated the $100 for the cornerstone, and "concluded the day's activities with a tasteful speech."[1]

Although neither Jarmulowsky's speech nor the speeches made by the other presenters are recorded—the congregational minute book mentions only that the speakers praised the congregation's "holy goals"—it would be surprising if they had not emphasized that the synagogue would be the first great house of worship built by east European Jews in New York—and in the United States. The growing east European Jewish population had formed congregations, but they

Cornerstone
By September 1886 the congregation had filed building plans with the New York Department of Buildings, and on November 14 it held a ceremony to celebrate the laying of the cornerstone. Photograph by Rachel Rabhan.

met in makeshift spaces: rented halls, converted storefronts, renovated churches. The picture of the synagogue printed in the *Yidishe gazeten* two days before the groundbreaking promised a striking structure with Moorish ornaments, finials, and stained-glass windows. If the newspaper article focused on the congregation's history and charitable nature—it mentioned fundraising for a talmudic academy in Russia—the speakers must have directed the congregants' thoughts forward to the day when they would worship in a structure built especially for Orthodox worship.[2] Over the previous few years, with the dramatic increase in the number of east European immigrants, small, society-like congregations had sprung up, filling nondescript halls and courtyards throughout the neighborhood. In setting the cornerstone for a structure that would seat 740, the congregation was setting a precedent for the east European Jews in America.

At least two of the congregants—Abba Baum and Joshua Rothstein—had been members of the congregation since the 1850s and could recall when the

The Building as Imagined
This drawing of the synagogue predates its
construction. The congregation included it in an 1887
advertisement in the *Yidishe gazeten* to recruit new members.

first east European congregation had formed in New York. In a Jewish population composed almost entirely of central European Jews, the tiny congregation directed its pioneering energies toward finding people who wished to pray and study according to the customs they had grown up with in Poland and Russia. At the time, the majority of New York's Jewish population lived slightly to the west of the Lower East Side, in a neighborhood called Five Points. The many Irish and German immigrants who lived there worked as laborers, artisans, and merchants. The central and east European Jews among them specialized in old clothing and glass. Because the immigrant Jews, like their neighbors, worked and lived in the same neighborhood, they naturally located their congregations in the neighborhood as well. In July 1852, Beth Hamedrash, the first Russian congregation in the United States, commenced services in a Bayard Street garret.[3]

The accommodations on Bayard Street were, at $8 a month, affordable. Congregants met to pray twice a day and also attended study sessions, led by a volunteer rabbi, Abraham Joseph Ash. After the High Holidays that first year, bolstered by an additional ten men, the congregation relocated to the first floor of a building on Elm Street, at the corner of Canal, renting it for $15 a month. The din of a carpentry shop directly above their new hall must have disturbed their prayers, however, because after Passover, 1853, the congregation moved again, this time to a former courthouse at Pearl Street and Center, renting the top floor for $25 a month. Although members had acquired a more expansive space, the new building's lower level housed a saloon, which probably would have been just as noisy, given that the standard workweek encompassed Saturday. Judah David Eisenstein, an early chronicler, speculated that the noise did not bother them; it is more likely that the congregation had no alternative. Lacking the resources to buy their own building, they were compelled to rent, and in a crowded neighborhood that was at once residential and commercial, most available halls were in stores and office buildings. Many congregations lacked their own buildings; as late as 1860, only six out of New York's twenty-seven congregations prayed in synagogues built as synagogues.[4]

As Beth Hamedrash moved from hall to hall, expanding its membership and formalizing its leadership structure, the east European congregation mirrored the central European congregations, especially with regard to absorption of American ideas.[5] In general, America's religious voluntarism made it difficult for congregational leadership to satisfy every individual member but, by the same token, made it very easy for groups to start their own congregations. Between 1825 and 1860, New York's congregations increased from one to twenty-seven. This dramatic increase was in part due to growing immigration, but it was primarily the product of factionalism and voluntarism. Members who tired of their congregations could start new ones. And if arriving immigrants found the current options unappealing, they, too, could start their own congregations. The members of Beth Hamedrash, by forming their own congregation rather than joining a preexisting one, thus — it could be said — demonstrated their Americanization.

Beth Hamedrash quickly distinguished itself as an east European congregation, one that strictly adhered to the conventions of Jewish law and study. Although many congregations in the 1850s were nominally traditional or Orthodox with regard to prayer, they were more lenient in practice. Beth Hamedrash's members devoted themselves to Jewish law, sought to import and train the proper functionaries to ensure the maintenance of the Orthodox standard, and cultivated the study of Jewish texts. Indeed, Beth Hamedrash was the first congregation in the history of New York in which "a group of Jews engaged in study for its own sake." In addition to Ash, members included several rabbis, a scribe, and a kosher slaughterer. The congregation housed a library of talmudic, rabbinic, and kabbalistic books and regularly offered Talmud classes and lectures. Before long, it became the most sought-after American authority on Jewish law; other congregations throughout the country sent their questions to Beth Hamedrash to be answered, and required its stamp of certification for their ritual slaughterers.[6]

Interestingly, its status as a standard-bearer for Jewish law improved its real-estate prospects. Normally a congregation took at least a decade to acquire its own property; Beth Hamedrash took a mere four years. John Hart, an uptown Jew in search of a place to recite kaddish, the traditional memorial prayer, for his father, came upon Beth Hamedrash and not only prayed there but studied a section of Torah and the Mishnah (Oral Law) with the rabbi. Impressed, Hart soon persuaded several fellow members of Shearith Israel, the Spanish and Portuguese synagogue, including the wealthy Samson Simpson, to contribute $4,000 toward the purchase of a Welsh church at 78 Allen Street for the young congregation. On June 8, 1856, the congregation held a dedication ceremony, with Abraham Rice, the first ordained rabbi in the country, delivering the sermon.[7]

Though pleased with the new building, the congregation was concerned about the permissibility of converting a church into a synagogue. While the Talmud does contain certain structural prescriptions—a synagogue should be tall, it should have windows, it should allow worshippers to face in the direction of Jerusalem for the eighteen benedictions, and the ark should be raised—it does not specify "forms and styles," for the emphasis of Jewish law and custom is on study. Despite this latitude and the precedent already established by central European Jews for converting churches into synagogues, Beth Hamedrash felt compelled to send queries to rabbinical authorities in eastern Europe: Was it acceptable to convert a formerly Christian house of worship into a Jewish one? The official response was reassuring: Protestant churches lacked iconography, so they were acceptable. Rabbi Yosef Natanson assured the congregation that worship at 78 Allen Street was permissible, and offered the added rationale that since the building had originally been constructed as a secular space and only later became a Protestant church, and because the congregation desired to worship there permanently, it had further justification for converting the space into a synagogue.[8]

The characterization of 78 Allen Street decades later as "a good spiritual and physical situation" can be attributed in no small part to its surroundings. With no saloon or carpentry shop for competition, the converted church could accommodate the needs of the growing congregation: "a brick building three stories and basement in height, twenty-five feet wide front and rear and about 70 feet deep."[9] Situated on a 25 by 87 1/2 foot lot, the building had a courtyard in which the congregation constructed a *mikvah*, or ritual bath. At Allen Street, Beth Hamedrash continued to cultivate its reputation as a major Orthodox congregation. Expanding the charitable services as well, members attended to the sick and formed a burial society.

Early in its tenure at Allen Street, the congregation survived an internal conflict that underscored the power of the laity. In 1859 a trivial dispute between the lay leader, President Joshua Rothstein, and followers of the rabbi, Abraham Ash, splintered the congregation, with Ash's faction electing a new president. The inevitable clash between the two presidents led to a court case, with the judge ruling in favor of Rothstein as the rightfully elected leader of an incorporated religious society. As a result, the twenty-three members who had sided with Ash left with their president and a stipulated $300 to form their own congregation. Though fewer in number than Beth Hamedrash, they incorporated as Beth Hamedrash Hagadol, "The Great House of Study." The court case indicates that the lay leaders had power and authority over the rabbi; this relationship was strong in America from the beginning and came to characterize east European synagogues in America. The strength of the lay leadership did not lead to an automatic dismissal of rabbinical authority, for at Allen Street the remaining forty-six members supported rabbinical scholarship and attracted some of the more learned and notable east European functionaries to come to the United States.[10] At the same time, the lay members did assert their dominance when conflicts arose. From this point on, preachers would be fired and cantors let go, but only death could remove an elected president from office.

Although the congregation flourished by all accounts, the "good spiritual and physical conditions" and peaceful atmosphere changed dramatically in 1878, when the Manhattan Transit Company commenced construction of the Second Avenue elevated railroad down Allen Street. The noise, vibrations, and discom-

fort caused by the construction and the eventual operation of the railroad moti-
vated the congregation to take the Manhattan Railway Company and the Metro-
politan Elevated Railway Company to court. The following description, offered
as testimony in the case, details the disturbances: "The said street, in front of said
premises, were darkened, and said premises bounded by said street were deprived
of light, air and ventilation and quiet, and passage along said street was and is
interrupted; access to said premises was and is now greatly impaired; ashes, cinders, oil, water and other substances were precipitated upon the street and sidewalk in front of said premises, and upon and against the building thereon erected
and its appurtenances and upon persons passing into and from said premises and
buildings and along said street, and noxious and disagreeable gases, smoke, steam,
ashes and cinders were constantly emitted by the engines upon said railroad passing said premises and penetrated into the street and into said premises and buildings and all such annoyances and trespasses continued."[11]

Not only did the railroad's construction and operation disrupt the services of
the congregation; it also made the synagogue less attractive to prospective members and affected the congregation's ability to rent rooms. Congregation leaders
must have considered leaving the premises in favor of a site where they could hold
Sabbath and weekday services with decorum. The earliest extant ledger books of
the congregation, which date to 1882, show the congregation's desire to promote
seemliness and order; to these ends, the leadership purchased spittoons and hired
policemen to control High Holiday crowds. Now the building shook and rained
soot on worshippers, which must have irked members, the more prominent of
whom now included bankers, real-estate agents, and other businessmen.

In the mid-1880s the congregation took steps to avoid the immediate dis-
ruption of the elevated railroad and to secure its own standing among the other
east European synagogues. As Beth Hamedrash's physical condition had deterio-
rated, several major congregations—including the offshoot congregation, Beth
Hamedrash Hagadol—had purchased much larger churches and held dedication
ceremonies, generating even more incentive for relocation. Seeing the success of
their counterparts must have rankled members of Beth Hamedrash. Indeed, one
uptown observer declared that it was the strong sense of competition with their
offshoot that resulted in the building of the Eldridge Street Synagogue: the syna-

gogue's "very existence emanated . . . from a spirit of jealousy towards . . . the Beth Hamedrash Hagadol." Although we do not know when or how the idea of building a synagogue came to Beth Hamedrash, President Sender Jarmulowsky must have begun conversations with Note Lubetkin, president of Holkhe Yosher Vizaner, "Those Who Walk in Righteousness," about a possible merger, the purchase of lots, and a new name in late 1885 or early 1886. On May 6, 1886, Beth Hamedrash sold 78 Allen to another congregation, Machsike Torah Sinier, for $19,000, a sale recorded in a ledger. Three weeks later, the congregation held a special meeting to announce that they had merged with Holkhe Yosher Vizaner. At this point, the merged congregation began to use the new name, Kahal Adath Jeshurun, but it did not legally change the name until 1890. *Kahal Adath Jeshurun* has been translated most often as "Community of the People of Israel," but given the original partner's name, Holkhe Yosher, the meaning probably intended was "People's Congregation of the Just." Indeed, that translation was still being used on court documents twenty years later. According to the terms of the merger, Beth Hamedrash (now referring to itself as Kahal Adath Jeshurun) acquired Holkhe Yosher's lots on 14 and 16 Eldridge Street. Kahal Adath Jeshurun soon purchased lot 12 as well.[12]

Once the leaders had arranged the mergers and secured the three contiguous lots, the next step was to hire architects. The congregation selected Peter and Francis William Herter, German immigrants who had arrived in New York several years earlier. The Herters had no experience in synagogue design; in fact, the synagogue was only their fifth commission in the city. It is quite probable that they, as Catholics, had never even entered a synagogue. What they did have, however, was experience building in the neighborhood; in 1886 they were in the midst of constructing two tenements down the block, at 43 and 45 Eldridge Street. Whether the congregation's leaders met them on Eldridge or at their offices— David A. Cohen, a member active on the building committee, had a realty firm, Golde and Cohen, at 198 Broadway, near Herter Brothers, at 191 Broadway—the collaboration formally began in July 1886 with the filing of the building plans.

We know remarkably little about the way the Herters went about designing the synagogue and the extent to which they collaborated with the congregation's leaders. The original architects' drawings no longer exist. Even the New Building Application, filed on July 12, 1886, and its amended version, filed on September 16, are not very helpful, as the former version specifies a central tower that was never built and the latter version lists Dorchester stone rather than brick as the main building material (brick was eventually used). Finances were probably responsible for these changes. Construction commenced on September 26, 1886, and the dedication ceremony was held a year later, on September 4.[13]

The Herters employed a combination of Gothic, Romanesque, and Moorish styles, but it was the Moorish influence that was most distinct in the finished structure. The Herters had probably encountered the Moorish style in Germany, where, in the mid-nineteenth century, synagogues first adopted it. Moorish synagogue architecture appealed to acculturating Jews for both ideological and practical reasons. Ideologically, it harked back to a relatively peaceful period in Jewish history, the Golden Age of Spain, in the tenth through twelfth centuries. Practically, it provided a way for Jews to distinguish their houses of worship from Christian churches, designed chiefly in the Gothic and Romanesque styles. By the time the Herters arrived in New York, they could see that the Moorish style had caught on in the United States as well. A flurry of synagogue construction immediately after the Civil War had produced some of the finest examples in New York City—most notably, Temple Emanu-El, on Fifth Avenue and Forty-third Street, and Central Synagogue, on Lexington Avenue and Fifty-fifth Street.[14]

The prominence of Temple Emanu-El as the standard-bearer of the Reform movement and certain structural similarities between the two synagogues have prompted speculation that Kahal Adath Jeshurun, an avowedly Orthodox congregation, had both ideological and aesthetic motivations for drawing architectural inspiration from it. Citing the similarities between Temple Emanu-El and the Eldridge Street Synagogue in proportion and design—the portal motives, pendant tower windows, rose window, crowning arcade—John Donald Stewart, one person who researched the Eldridge Street Synagogue, wrote, "It is tempting to assume that Kahal Adath Jeshurun wanted a downtown building rivaling the much feared reform synagogue in grandeur." In adopting the grand elements of the design, perhaps Kahal Adath Jeshurun intended to project a message that a

Facade Watercolor
    The synagogue's eclectic combination of Moorish, Gothic, and Romanesque styles contrasted with the workaday styles of neighboring shops and tenements. This watercolor and pencil drawing, probably produced by the architectural firm Herter Brothers in 1886, predates the construction of the synagogue. Museum of the City of New York, The J. Clarence Davies Collection.

Jew could acculturate and remain Orthodox.[15] If so, we can consider the Moorish facades—one on Fifth Avenue and one on Eldridge Street—to be in a sort of conversation with each other about the ways to blend Americanization and Judaism.

Other speculation about the design of the building has centered on the windows, arches, bays, and doors as reflecting the architects' attention to Jewish numerology. It is suggested that the congregants influenced the design. If we follow this train of thought, the Gothic rose window, an architectural element usually associated with a church, would signify the twelve tribes of Israel because of the twelve rondelles around its circumference. The five horseshoe windows

Restored Rose Window
A Gothic element, the rose window on the west wall of the synagogue, commonly reminds visitors of a Catholic church. One story has it that the architects lent this window a Jewish cast by adding the twelve outer rondelles, representing the twelve tribes of Israel. Photograph © 2007 by Kate Milford.

below it would represent the five books of Moses; the three bays of the building, the Patriarchs, Abraham, Isaac, and Jacob; and the four doors, the Matriarchs, Sarah, Rebecca, Leah, and Rachel.

Whether this numerical connection — or the architectural similarities to Temple Emanu-El, for that matter — was planned or coincidental, the building was costly to construct and ornament. The congregation's ledger book itemizes the various sums paid for the lots to build on and to the masons, carpenters, and architects, which totaled $91,907.61 — a considerable expenditure. The new building cost almost five times the amount the congregation had received for the Allen Street property. Beth Hamedrash Hagadol's purchase and conversion of the Norfolk Street Methodist Episcopal Church cost $55,000.[16]

The large sums spent to build the synagogue drew ire from some contemporary observers. The same year construction commenced on Eldridge Street, Rabbi Moses Weinberger, a rabbi from Hungary, wrote a commentary on Jews and Juda-

R. H. Casey Bill

The many charges accrued in the construction of the synagogue are itemized in the congregation's ledger. This 1888 bill from the carpenter and builder R. H. Casey lists costs adding up to nearly $18,000, a significant portion of the $91,907 total.

ism in New York. Weinberger was displeased with the state of American religious life in general; he decried the lack of respect accorded rabbis, the desecration of the Sabbath, and congregations' misplaced priorities. He was especially critical of the amount of money that congregations spent on their buildings: "The lust for . . . larger, more magnificent synagogues reaching up even into the heavens—took hold suddenly among congregations and societies and has in recent days developed in the most awesome fashion. It has led to a great deal of evil and taken our people ten steps backward."[17] The timing of Weinberger's publication—concurrent with the opening of the Eldridge Street Synagogue—suggests that Weinberger had the Eldridge Street Synagogue in mind when he penned his words.

If he found fault with the construction bills, he saw great promise in the rise of *mitzvah* merchants, and the Eldridge Street Synagogue certainly encouraged this American trend. A *mitzvah* is a commandment, or religious obligation, and a mitzvah merchant was someone who sold religious articles (books, Sab-

K. Paston's Bookstore and Business Card
    Kalmon Paston established his religious bookstore at 18 Eldridge Street in 1887, the year that the congregation opened its new synagogue. The business stayed in the family into the 1970s. Judge Paul P. E. Bookson, Paston's grandson, was the lay leader of the congregation from the 1970s until his death in 2004, and his wife, Tova, and their children and grandchildren still worship at the synagogue. Tax Photographs. Courtesy NYC Municipal Archives (store); Collection of the Museum at Eldridge Street (card).

bath candlesticks, Passover matzos) or performed religious services (marriages, divorces, ritual circumcisions). Mitzvah merchants made the traditional observances more accessible to the masses. Even before the Eldridge Street Synagogue was completed, it attracted to the neighborhood businessmen and businesswomen who banked on the synagogue's power to draw in customers. Next door to the synagogue, at 18 Eldridge, Kalmon Paston opened Paston's Judaica, in 1887. There, Paston's family sold religious goods, such as prayer shawls, Sabbath candlesticks, and Hebrew texts. Moshe Ziskind Feinsilber, a religious functionary and ritual circumciser, moved from Bayard Street to 41 Eldridge just in time for the opening of the synagogue.[18] Around the corner, Gittel Natelson's mikvah, for ritual bathing, helped make that traditional Jewish observance for women not only possible but appealing.

    As a businesswoman—mikvah attendant, wigmaker, and real-estate investor—as well as the holder of balcony seat 20 in the Eldridge Street Synagogue,

Gittel Natelson combined both religious knowledge and a developing understanding of business opportunities in America. Working with her husband, Isaac, Gittel Natelson bought property and advertised in the Yiddish newspapers to create a business that served both secular and religious needs. Preserving Judaism in urban America required adaptation and innovation, and the Natelsons' business trajectory shows how they were able to take the role of religious functionaries, employees of a congregation, and branch off to create their own business.

In the spring of 1886, both Gittel and Isaac were employed at the Beth Hamedrash synagogue at 78 Allen Street, Isaac as *shames*, or sexton; Gittel as mikvah attendant. When the congregation sold the building, as well as the mikvah, to Machsike Torah Sinier, the Natelsons established their own bath and mikvah business near the soon-to-be-built Kahal Adath Jeshurun synagogue. In the summer of 1886, Isaac purchased the lot around the corner from the construction site for the Eldridge Street Synagogue, at 5 Allen Street, and the Natelsons announced that their "kosher mikvah" had "moved, moved, moved" in their September 1886 advertisement. The announcement featured Gittel's name and established her credibility by noting her prior management of the mikvah at Beth Hamedrash and her husband's role as sexton. It also mentions that she was a "wigmaker."[19] For reasons of modesty, many Orthodox women do not show their own hair after marriage and customarily wear wigs.

The Natelsons displayed business acumen not only in capitalizing on their knowledge of the congregation's new site to build a mikvah but also in combining a secular bathhouse with the mikvah business. The New York City directory soon listed the establishment as the Allen Street Baths, seemingly a secular bathhouse and steam room for men. But in a local newspaper, the *Yidishe gazeten*, an advertisement listed the same address for a mikvah and for secular baths for women. Having paid $22,000 for the lot and the building, the Natelsons doubtless invested much more to construct baths to serve the different sets of customers. The investment proved worthwhile, for the dual business persisted into the 1940s.[20]

Neither the advertisement nor the minutes of the Beth Hamedrash mention any connection between the synagogue and Gittel Natelson's mikvah, yet there does seem to have been an arrangement, albeit informal, between the parties. Prior

Allen Street Baths

The bathhouse established by Gittel and Isaac Natelson at 5 Allen Street in 1886 offered a secular bathhouse for men and a "fine" mikvah (*Yidishe gazeten*, October 14, 1887). The Natelsons retired in 1902, but the bathhouse remained open for business into the 1940s. The Hebrew sign above the south door in this 1940 photograph reads, "Kosher Mikvah, for all daughters of Israel"; the English sign above the north door reads, "Russian and Turkish baths." Tax Photographs. Courtesy NYC Municipal Archives.

to the move, the congregation had maintained the mikvah at 78 Allen, arranging for repairs and paying the Natelsons. Had the Natelsons not had an arrangement with Beth Hamedrash to support them at their new location, they could have remained with the new congregation at 78 Allen Street, Machsike Torah Sinier, or purchased a lot elsewhere. Isaac's $100 deposit for seats for his family at the Eldridge Street Synagogue, made in December 1886, and the lack of a provision for a mikvah at the Eldridge Street site support the connection. Both the congregation and the Natelsons stood to benefit. The congregation had a mikvah directly behind its synagogue but was free of the responsibility and costs of its maintenance. In turn, the Natelsons had a guaranteed clientele among their fellow members at the synagogue and had their own business. The Natelsons' direct control shows that the congregation was stepping back from mikvah administration, ceding some of the ancillary synagogue functions to mitzvah merchants.

Advertisements in the Yiddish papers suggest the Natelsons were pioneers in opening a mikvah that did not operate under the aegis of a congregation. An 1884 survey lists fifteen mikvahs in New York, each connected to a congregation. By the time the Natelsons' mikvah opened, the Yiddish press had identified at least four mikvahs on the Lower East Side, all of them in competition with one another and under the management of a congregation. The Hungarian mikvah on Attorney Street was associated with the Anshe Sfard congregation and was listed as the "most kosher," with "all the best improvements." The 78 Allen Street mikvah, associated with Machsike Torah Sinier and managed by a Mr. Baranovski, was the "oldest" and had "all the comforts and cleanliness." At the Kol Israel Anshe Polin mikvah at 80 Forsyth Street, a visitor could enjoy "all the best comforts" without "waiting in line." The Natelsons' facilities enjoyed success; within a year Gittel and Isaac had added four baths, making theirs, with eighteen baths and two "splendid" mikvahs, the largest of all mikvah businesses appearing in contemporary advertisements. The Natelsons' advertisement in the fall of 1887 stated that "no mikvah in New York is as fine" as theirs. The language of the advertisements indicates that immigrant women were interested both in rabbinical certification and a bath boasting "all of the best improvements."[21]

As a mitzvah merchant, Gittel Natelson provided an important religious service for women who wanted to live an Orthodox Jewish life in America. The construction of baths "represented an initial attempt by the multitude of newcomers to preserve Judaism in urban America." According to Jewish law and custom, women's monthly attendance at the mikvah supersedes synagogue attendance in importance, as do kindling Sabbath candles and preparing the Sabbath hallah (braided bread).[22] The city directory listing of the 5 Allen Street establishment only as a secular bathhouse suggests that there may have been many mikvahs combined with other commercial enterprises. This is especially significant for historians and sociologists who have looked at the apparent lack of mikvahs as evidence of a decline in religious life. The success of the Natelsons' business suggests that many women continued to visit mikvahs even as they Americanized.

After the cornerstone for the new synagogue was laid, the parade-goers went on with their daily lives: working, selling, shopping, raising families. Gradually the neighborhood was being transformed — most dramatically by the magnificent new synagogue under construction but more subtly by the sprouting up of new businesses that made the immigrants' religion easier to observe. Now there were immigrants like Kalmon Paston, with his religious bookstore, and Gittel Natelson, with her wigmaking and mikvah, as well as Kalmon London, treasurer of a newly formed yeshiva, Etz Chaim, who later went into the kosher matzo business, and the widow Esther Sokolski, whose husband, Chaim, had been a leading member of Beth Hamedrash beginning in the mid-1850s and the founder of Sokolski's religious bookstore. Twenty years after the cornerstone ceremony, Peter Wiernik, editor of the Orthodox Yiddish newspaper *Morgn zhurnal*, underscored the financial success of Jewish bookstores, the aggregate income of Jewish functionaries, and the "millions of dollars invested in synagogue real estate" as proof of American Judaism's vitality.[23] But in 1887 the experiment of the east European immigrant Jews in building a grand synagogue devoted to Orthodox Judaism was just beginning, and it symbolized tensions and controversies in American Jewry that the parade-goers were unlikely to have imagined.

THREE

Opening Day

ON SEPTEMBER 4, 1887, less than ten months after the cornerstone-laying ceremony, congregation members returned to Eldridge Street, joined this time by throngs of downtown residents and uptown observers eager to participate in the new synagogue's dedication. Some of those in attendance had received formal invitations—the building committee had dispatched "thousands" of them—and others were caught up in the excitement generated by the gathering crowds. According to one newspaper, "an immense number of people" converged on Eldridge Street that afternoon, so many that "the crowds extended to the street, and order was difficult to maintain."[1]

As people waited to enter the synagogue, they could observe how the building, with its grandeur and scale, contrasted with neighborhood workshops, tenements, and even synagogues. Most downtown Jewish congregations of the day were hidden away in ordinary tenement halls, many of which lacked distinctive facades and none of which announced their presence the way the Eldridge Street Synagogue did. Even the largest Jewish congregations on the Lower East Side, such as Beth Hamedrash Hagadol and Ohab Zedek, convened in buildings originally designed as churches. The Eldridge Street Synagogue's elaborate Star of David patterns, set in terra-cotta bands and carved on the heavy wooden doors, consequently announced a new type of Lower East Side structure. Although the prominent rose window echoed those of many a Christian church, the Moorish cast of the surrounding keyhole-shaped windows, the horseshoe arches, and the

Facade after Restoration

The facade after its restoration, completed in 2006, looks much the way it appeared to the crowds at the dedication ceremony in 1887. Photograph © 2006 by Kate Milford.

Terra-Cotta Star

The synagogue exterior has Stars of David cast in terra cotta. The first set of building plans filed in July 1886 specified the use of Dorchester stone, but in the revised plans filed in 1887, brick and terra-cotta ornamentation replaced the carved stone, which was more expensive. Photograph by Diane Kaese.

roofline's marvelous lacy finials boldly distinguished it from neighborhood Jewish houses of prayer and also from churches attended by the local Irish, Italians, and Germans.

In a city, and even country, in which most new synagogues were designed as Reform temples, the dedication of a beautiful new Orthodox synagogue carried a weighty symbolism and drew the attention of journalists who shared their impressions with readers throughout the country. If the cornerstone ceremony was a point at which Kahal Adath Jeshurun privately assessed its past and raised funds for the future building, the dedication of the synagogue was a public event, the implications and interpretations of which reverberated far beyond the Lower East Side. As one historian puts it, "In a dramatically concrete way the immigrants established a place for themselves within the American religious landscape and paved the way for their American-born children to follow in their footsteps."[2]

Remarkably, the congregation's "special events ledger," which devotes a paragraph to the cornerstone-laying event, is relatively silent on the subject of the dedication, using the space instead for a hastily written itemization of the general costs of the building. It was the less glamorous aspects of opening a synagogue—paying bills, hiring a choir, selling seats—that consumed the leaders' time, and in the flurry of making arrangements for the dedication, they had little time for reflection. Even the announcement of the dedication ceremony in the *Yidishe gazeten* emphasized post-dedication matters, such as how to buy or rent a seat, more than the "famous" speakers at the ceremony.[3]

Reports by contemporary observers representing both American and Jewish publications yield considerably more information about opening day than do the congregation's archives. According to the *New York Herald*, the dedication ceremony began with the chanting of psalms, after which Nathan Hutkoff, chair of the building committee, had the honor of lighting the eternal light. The ceremony achieved its high point when Isidor Abrahams "threw open the doors" of the ark, and the Torah was "solemnly deposited in its crimson lined sanctuary." After the recitation of additional psalms, a series of speakers ascended to the lectern. By the time President Sender Jarmulowsky gave his closing address, nearly four hours had passed.

Although the account in the *Herald* is straightforward, several Jewish publications representing various denominational viewpoints delivered accounts with strong doses of opinion. The congregants' behavior, immigrant Orthodoxy, and religious leadership all earned comments. The reactions cast into relief the competition among the Reform, Conservative, and Orthodox movements, as well as class conflicts between uptown and downtown Jews. By 1887 the majority of the synagogues of the central European Jews that dotted uptown neighborhoods had embraced Reform Judaism. Although the congregations had started as traditional, immigrant groups in the 1850s and 1860s, over time they had grown lax in their ritual observances, and synagogue leaders had responded with a variety of reforms designed to make Judaism mesh with members' occupational and social needs and aspirations. They abridged services, incorporated more English and German translations, adopted family seating, and aimed for a "refined and pleasing ritual."[4]

In 1885 a convention of leading Reform rabbis issued the Pittsburgh Platform, which provided an ideological rationale for Reform Judaism. This document emphasized Jewish morals and ethics and declared that Jewish ritual law was no longer binding. In 1886 several Orthodox rabbis and leaders of what became a third movement, Conservative Judaism, established a rabbinical school, the Jewish Theological Seminary, which acknowledged the importance of training new rabbis in "English culture" and the "American spirit" but, unlike the Reform movement, upheld the importance of Jewish law, the "strong historical armor of historical Judaism."[5] Despite the variations among the movements, the proponents of each believed their form of Judaism to be best suited for America and hoped that the east European Jews or, more to the point, their children would swell the ranks of their denomination.

Although the Reform temples were located uptown, beyond the Jewish quarter, fear of the Reform movement was evident at the Eldridge Street Synagogue on opening day. Two uptown rabbis, Henry Pereira Mendes of the Shearith Israel Congregation, the oldest congregation in New York, atypical in its retention of Orthodoxy, and Bernard Drachman, an American-born Orthodox rabbi, traveled to the Lower East Side and ascended to the lectern to deliver commemorative speeches. That two uptown Orthodox rabbis would take such an interest in their downtown coreligionists' new synagogue and that the downtown congregation so eagerly sought their guidance suggests that the city's Orthodox Jews felt the need to forge alliances. Mendes implored his listeners to instruct their children "in the teachings of religion" and make them "familiar with Jewish history" lest they, "in growing up, leave the synagogue and join the temples up town." Drachman pleaded with the assembled Jews to maintain their traditions, or else "they might stand before their mirrors some morning and not recognize themselves as orthodox anymore." These speeches targeted the Reform movement, not apostasy, as the looming threat and reminded listeners that an adherence to traditional observances would be needed to make their synagogue a true "battlement" against Reform.[6]

Reform observers seemed just as anxious as the Orthodox rabbis that day. Within the past five years, the arrival of tens of thousands of east European Jews on America's shores and their formation of hundreds of Orthodox congregations had challenged Reform's preeminence. Now, as the historian Leon Jick points out, "the Reform congregations, which for a brief time had considered that they represented the totality of American Jewry and the future of American Judaism, found themselves a minority on the margins of communal life."[7] The construction of the Eldridge Street Synagogue, dedicated to Orthodoxy, concretized the fear that Orthodox Judaism would supplant Reform as *the* form of American Judaism.

A journalist, Mi Yodea, from the Cincinnati-based Reform publication *American Israelite,* depicted the dedication ceremony as if to assuage the fears of his nationwide Reform readers. According to Mi Yodea, the Eldridge Street Synagogue met the Reform movement's expectations for a pleasing setting in which to worship. He extolled the "elegant simplicity" of the building and the sense of spaciousness and light and observed how the "massive pillars which support the gallery lend a feeling of security to the visitor, and give him no cause for the feeling of oppression and uneasiness which usually overcomes one amidst the throng in a crowded public building." Mi Yodea's kind words came at a heavy price, however, for he employed this description as a setup for devastating criticism. He wrote, "I wish I could speak as favorably of the dedication exercises as of the place in which they were held," then gave a litany of the grievously indecorous acts of the congregants: women sparring over a balcony seat, "gentlemen" who retained their cigar stumps with the intention of smoking them on the street after the dedication, and babies incessantly crying. He also mentioned "loud talking" during the ceremony and "the running to and fro of the trustees as well as the public during the lectures and singing." The congregation had attempted to control the crowds by positioning trustees throughout the sanctuary who could signal the shames if the crowds became too noisy. Upon receiving a signal, the shames would thump the reading table with his fist "and a sort of small thunder reverberated through the synagogue."[8] Mi Yodea noted how futile the thumping proved: "The old noise reasserted itself" soon enough, requiring recurrent thumping throughout the dedication ceremony.

The chattiness and restlessness that day are perhaps explained by the ceremony's four-hour length and the incomprehensibility of the English speeches to a good portion of the Yiddish-speaking audience. Mi Yodea offered his own explanation, arguing that the immigrants' lack of decorum in the house of God might "be attributed to the fact that they visit it too often and thus consider it almost their second home, which they can enter not only *en négligé,* but in which they can demean themselves *sans gêne.*" Since this was the first time the congregation had gathered together in their new synagogue, when Mi Yodea said they visited the synagogue "too often," he seemed to be implying a criticism not just of the congregants of the Eldridge Street Synagogue but of east European and Orthodox Jews' observances in general. He concluded with the pronouncement that the immigrants' Old World sensibility would ultimately render them unable to hire an Americanized Orthodox leader like Drachman or Mendes: "A modern minister at

Barrel-Vaulted Ceiling
     The fifty-foot-high barrel-vaulted ceiling lends a sense of spaciousness to the sanctuary, which in its heyday accommodated more than one thousand worshippers on High Holidays. Photograph © 2007 by Kate Milford.

the head of such a congregation would have about the same effect as a handsome new silk velvet collar on an old threadbare coat." Despite the solidity and staying power conveyed by the edifice, Mi Yodea implied that it was still Reform Judaism, with its emphasis on abbreviated services, its inspiring sermons, and its focus on contemporary meaning, that was needed to curtail indecorous behavior and ensure that the "modern," "new," and "handsome" American setting would attract future generations. In other words, Orthodox Judaism itself was "threadbare" and would not survive the changes wrought in the new environment.

If the *American Israelite*, through Mi Yodea, praised the architecture but criticized the retention of tradition, the *American Hebrew* criticized the congregation's attention to outward trappings to the neglect of traditional values. A letter to the editor by the educator Adolph Benjamin, writing under a pseudonym (Ish Yemini), decried the amount of money and time spent on bricks and mortar at the expense of more pressing spiritual matters: "Is this the orthodoxy which we should strive to bequeath to our children? A Judaism composed of carved wood and ornamented bricks and covered up by a handsome mortgage is all that will be left for them to liquidate." He disparaged the effort by downtown congregations—including the Eldridge Street Synagogue—to import an east European rabbi to lead them. Their fractiousness and divisiveness would cause the project to "evaporate into air." Rather than spend money on a synagogue or a chief rabbi, Benjamin urged his fellow downtown Jews to support educational endeavors.[9]

In promoting religious education, Benjamin and the *American Hebrew* appear to have had as an ulterior motive the promotion of the Jewish Theological Seminary, which they apparently thought should have been the beneficiary of east European Jews' organizational and fundraising activity. Having just celebrated its own dedication that January, the seminary aspired to reach immigrant children in need of religious education and to soon provide the type of rabbinical leadership that its supporters believed was needed on the Lower East Side: leadership with "a civilizing power that will inevitably tend to elevate many of the vast throngs of our brethren who have no access to cultural forces." To educate their children, "the future pillars of American Judaism," the east European Jews would need to stop building frivolous synagogues and abandon their goal of importing east European rabbis; instead, the *American Hebrew* argued, they should "liberally contribut[e] toward the Seminary."[10]

At a time when Reform rabbis were lamenting empty pews and the Jewish Theological Seminary was searching for prospective rabbinical students and eventual positions for graduates, the downtown masses and their zest for religious services held a certain fascination for their uptown coreligionists. Indeed, the uptown *Jewish Messenger* trumpeted the crowds at the Eldridge Street Synagogue, commending the enthusiasm of the congregants on dedication day and, in a followup report, noting their continued devotion to prayer services there. Eldridge Street Synagogue services attracted such large crowds that club-wielding policemen were necessary to prevent chaos, and this was just for regular weekday services. "Up-town people have no idea of the throngs of Jews that attend synagogue services in the hundred and more shrines located below Second street. At one synagogue lately in Eldridge street, where there is accommodation for two thousand people, and at every evening service every seat was occupied, a line of policemen had to clear the street every few minutes, as hundreds tried to climb over the gates and crowd in, and only vigorous clubbing held them at bay."[11]

The *Yidishe gazeten*, the weekend edition of the prominent Yiddish newspaper *Yidishe tageblat*, challenged uptown notions about downtown Jews in its account of the congregation and its history. In a decade in which the east European population in New York dramatically increased, causing, as the *American Hebrew*, the *American Israelite*, and the *Jewish Messenger* all noted, the formation of numerous congregations, the *Yidishe gazeten* called Kahal Adath Jeshurun a proud example of what Americanized east European congregations would look like with time. Perhaps by design, its emphasis on the congregation's longevity and stability challenged the critics' characterization of downtown congregations' ever-splintering factions. The *Gazeten* celebrated the venerable history of the congregation, explaining that Kahal Adath Jeshurun was the former Beth Hamedrash on Allen Street and, as such, was the "oldest Orthodox community in New York." Although it commented that the synagogue itself was "beautiful" and "magnificent," it focused mainly on the congregation, finding that it was "worthy of sitting in this synagogue": "In this congregation they have never heard of division or conflict, there a peace and tranquility rule. The fact that, in the course of thirty years, this congregation has now only its sixth president is proof enough."[12] As we have seen, this description elides some major conflicts — some of which, in early years, had been addressed in American courts, and the most significant of which had resulted in the break-off congregation of Beth Hamedrash Hagadol. What takes precedence in this account was that an east European congregation had persevered and stabilized and now made a solid contribution to the city and the latest wave of immigrants.

The editor of the *Gazeten*, Kasriel Sarasohn, both supported Orthodoxy and evinced a certain downtown pride, praising the Eldridge Street Synagogue with words that must have been sincere, for he became a member of the congregation in the 1890s. In his account he held up the Eldridge Street Synagogue as a model to assure fellow east European Jews that if they formed honorable, peaceful congregations, they, too, could one day occupy a magnificent building. Sarasohn made special note of President Jarmulowsky's "splendid" speech, contrasting it with Rabbi Mendes' lecture, apparently repeated from another recent communal event. Sarasohn said that downtown Jews did not need "uptown rabbis" for such events. Even though Sarasohn praised the architecture and the world-famous cantor, he, like the *American Israelite* and the *American Hebrew*, underscored what was missing. Only when "the congregation also hires a rabbi, can one say 'and the braided thread will not unravel.'"[13]

The Eldridge Street Synagogue's congregation seemed to be more cognizant of the pressing communal and congregational issues of rabbinical leadership, decorum, and education than its commentators conceded. The most trenchant critique was the one expressed by Mi Yodea with regard to decorum. While he convincingly portrayed the service as cacophonous and the congregation as unruly, what cannot be denied is that in assigning trustees to control the crowd, the leadership was attempting to reinforce, if somewhat provisionally, a sense of decorum. And although the congregation employed a cantor and not a rabbi, they were in the process of uniting with Beth Hamedrash Hagadol and other leading east European congregations to form the Association of Orthodox Hebrew Congregations (Agudes ha-Kehillos) to import an east European rabbi. Indeed, President Jarmulowsky served as treasurer of the association, and the congregation pledged the second-highest yearly sum in support of the endeavor. Formally, the association's contract forbade its constituent congregations from hiring individual rabbis for their congregations, only preachers and cantors.[14] On a larger level, in opting to hire a communal rabbi, they took what they viewed to be the first step in countering the increasing obstacles that secular matters — business, education, entertainment — posed to traditional Judaism by attempting to re-create east European Orthodoxy and institutionalize, in some form, Jewish law.

The association succeeded in importing Rabbi Jacob Joseph as chief rabbi but was unable to institutionalize the desired Orthodox communal framework. Concern over rabbinical leadership continued to preoccupy Eldridge Street congregants, and they wrestled with larger communal organizational issues over the years. Like the classrooms of the Jewish Theological Seminary and the pews of the prominent uptown Reform temples, the Eldridge Street Synagogue's lofty sanctuary hosted American Jewish debates over the proper way to blend "American currents of thought" with Jewish tradition, as one observer put it. Although writers and speakers commenting on the new synagogue suggested a range of priorities and solutions, they all attested to the energy with which leaders of the various movements engaged in both preservation and Americanization. The opening of the building signified a major step for downtown Jews and their desire to preserve tradition, but, as Adolph Benjamin said in a letter to the editor of the *American Hebrew*, he wanted to echo the sentiments of Rabbis Drachman and Mendes, "who urged that its members should not consider their laborious task complete, but as yet begun; to try to perpetuate our pure religion through the rising generation."[15] In the coming years, the Eldridge Steet Synagogue did just that, in the process defining their own solutions to the question of blending American currents of thought with traditional Judaism.

While Mi Yodea, Benjamin, Mendes, and Sarasohn attended the dedication ceremonies with a journalistic eye for trends or for an overview of the way the synagogue affected American Judaism, it is safe to assume that most in attendance were not as deeply invested in the debates. Many people came to admire the synagogue. Miles from Fifth Avenue's Temple Emanu-El and at a great spiritual remove from Reform Judaism, most of the Yiddish-speaking audience, even if they understood English, would have been puzzled by Rabbi Drachman's pleas for the erection of a battlement for Orthodoxy, when not a single Reform congregation existed south of Houston Street. What they could appreciate, however, was the way the Eldridge Street Synagogue provided a haven from the crowdedness of the neighborhood.

The quickening pace and expanding scale of the east European immigration had been changing the Lower East Side's landscape, for the three-story buildings inhabited by the previous immigrants, the Germans and the Irish, could not contain the population increase; this spurred the relentless rise of six-story tenements. Formerly a "quiet residential neighborhood," Eldridge Street became "a bustling and dense thoroughfare."[16] Although three-story buildings remained on either side of the synagogue, the rise of tenements on the west side of Eldridge Street, as well as the elevated railroads immediately to the east, on Allen Street, and to the south, on Division Street, contributed to the dynamically changing nature of the street.

Even with the expansion of tenement space upward, the buildings were still overcrowded. They typically had a store or two at ground level and families, small sweatshops, meeting halls, and even congregations housed on the upper floors. By 1890 the block north of Eldridge—bound by Eldridge, Canal, Hester and Forsyth Streets—was home to 2,628 people. The crowding made for unexpected living, working, and praying arrangements: a single tenement apartment could hold tailors by day and a family and boarders by night; a Thursday night dance hall could be swiftly transformed into a Friday night prayer hall.[17] In 1888 the *American Magazine* provided descriptions of tenements on several Lower East Side streets, including Eldridge: "They are great prison-like structures of brick, with narrow doors and steep rickety stairs." Housing and workspace on the Lower East Side remained infamous for insufficient light and air circulation. East Siders lived and worked in "buildings hastily constructed by speculators, which soon became synonymous with grinding poverty and a squalid existence."[18] To be sure, the wealthier members of the Eldridge Street Synagogue, such as Nathan Hutkoff, Sender Jarmulowsky, and Isaac Gellis, lived in fine brownstones along East Broadway and Henry Street, but the majority of the members occupied crowded tenements. One early congregant of the Eldridge Street Synagogue, Gussie Dubrin, recalled her mother's sense of disappointment with the family's new apartment on Rutgers Street: "It was a small apartment. My mother hated it. She was used to the country and fresh air." The writer Anzia Yezierska describes a newly arrived immigrant looking out a tenement window, only to face the brick wall of the next building, and asking, "Where's the sunshine in America?"[19]

During the peak of east European immigration, most Lower East Side places of worship, housed in the very same buildings and sometimes the very same rooms used for daily work and life, offered little reprieve from the cramped and dark quarters that were the norm. So well did they blend into the Lower East Side streetscape that a *New York Daily Tribune* reporter assigned to write about the "Hebrew quarter's" synagogues in 1896 had to seek them out: "Scores, and even hundreds, of tiny synagogues [are] hidden away in this region of old buildings — synagogues consisting of a single floor, or at the most two, and giving no sign of their existence until they are stumbled upon. Some of the older tenements, dark of stairway and almost crumbling with age, have two, three and even four of these little worshipping places within their walls, where prayers are said thrice daily." One such building, at 27 Ludlow Street, housed multiple congregations. Although the tenement's facade presented a typical five-story building, no fewer than five congregations divided up the three middle floors with the help of "cheap, rough" partitions, a bar room occupied the first floor, and a workshop filled the fifth. The *New York Times* reporter who explored that building said that during the holidays a building that should reasonably accommodate no more than two hundred worshippers held twelve hundred to fifteen hundred. Another contemporary observer noted that most of the more than one hundred synagogues that he surveyed were not "anything more than halls or large rooms in tenement-houses, sometimes above or below a drinking-place, and in a few instances in a ball-room, which on Saturdays puts off its unholy garb."[20]

The Eldridge Street Synagogue's expansive window-filled facade offered a powerful contrast to the squalid, dark neighborhood spaces. Those who ventured inside, as did hundreds on September 4, 1887, and thousands later, gained a singular impression of light and space. As we have seen, the spaciousness of the 3,060-square-foot sanctuary astounded even uptown visitors. The purchase of three lots for one building had allowed for a free-standing structure with sufficient space between it and its neighbors. Windows on every wall of the sanctuary admitted abundant sunlight, which filtered through sixty-seven red, turquoise, and gold

Stained-Glass Window
    Sixty-seven stained-glass windows, using the Star of
David as the main motif, add color — turquoise, gold, red — to the
sanctuary. The restorer, Gil's Studio, salvaged more than 85 percent
of the original glass. Photograph © 2007 by Kate Milford.

stained-glass windows. The focal point of the room, the walnut ark, paralleled the
shape of the facade, but with beautiful carving instead of the facade's terra-cotta
ornamentation and with azure tablets inscribed with the Ten Commandments in
gold instead of the facade's rose window. Above, wooden finials completed the
pattern.

    At the time of its dedication, the Eldridge Street Synagogue was the Lower
East Side's architectural Sabbath. According to Jewish tradition, the Sabbath

Ark

The elaborately carved walnut ark, the focus of the sanctuary, follows the shape of the facade. Inside the ark the same crimson velvet there on opening day lines a three-tiered platform accommodating twenty-four Torah scrolls. Photograph by Edward Cheng.

should be a day apart from all other days, with Jews abstaining from work in order to concentrate on spiritual matters and enhancing the day with special foods and clothes. The Eldridge Street Synagogue, in line with that tradition, provided a space that was unlike the average workshop, home, or even place of worship, and its distinctiveness increased as escalating immigration made the Lower East Side even more crowded and as the synagogue's space, light, and style offered a proportionately greater contrast with its surroundings. Eventually other congregations

Church-Synagogue with Finials
In 1898 a Jewish congregation bought this Gothic church and converted it into a synagogue. The finials that the congregation added bear a striking resemblance to the finials of the Eldridge Street Synagogue. Drawing by W. A. Rogers. Reproduced from E. S. Martin, "East Side Considerations," *Harper's New Monthly Magazine*, May 1898, p. 859.

built new synagogues of comparable scale and grandeur close to the Eldridge Street Synagogue: in 1892 the congregation Kol Israel Anshe Polin erected its own Byzantine-style synagogue around the corner on Forsyth Street, in 1903 the Congregation Sons of Israel Kalwarier built its Greco-Roman–style synagogue on nearby Pike Street, and the same year the Jassy congregation constructed their eclectic synagogue at 60 Rivington. Each of these structures left its own imprint on the Lower East Side streetscape. But even with the addition of these synagogues and the grand converted churches of Beth Hamedrash and the Bialystoker shul, such large, sun-drenched spaces were rare.

The style of the Eldridge Street Synagogue influenced the architecture of subsequent neighborhood synagogues. As new structures were being built expressly as synagogues, immigration meant the formation of still more congregations in an already crowded neighborhood and the conversion of former Protestant churches into synagogues. In 1898, *Harper's New Monthly Magazine* featured a drawing of a Gothic church with the caption "A synagogue that was once a church." The writer of the article, E. S. Martin, observed that when Jewish congregations acquired churches, they made exterior changes, "adorn[ing the church] with just enough Hebrew architecture to make its change of owners and uses apparent." Since the adornments added to the churches that Martin mentioned were finials that, as the historian David Kaufman has pointed out, were unmistakably modeled after those of Eldridge Street, it would appear that the Lower East Side "Hebrew architecture" referred to here belonged to the Eldridge Street Synagogue.[21]

Whether architectural or ideological, reverberations from the Eldridge Street Synagogue's dedication ceremony continued to be felt for decades. Newly arrived immigrants clamored to attend services, and more-established Americanizing members who had moved out of the Lower East Side retained their membership, hesitant to abandon their ties to such a glorious space. The congregation's leaders made the maintenance of the synagogue's architectural beauty a priority. But besides serving as building caretakers, they attended to the spiritual issues that their congregation confronted: synagogue leadership, the role of the rabbi, children's education, and matters of decorum. The first order of business—bringing over one of Europe's leading cantors, Pinhas Minkowsky—involved both leadership and decorum.

FOUR

Music and Money

LESS THAN TWO WEEKS after the dedication ceremony, Cantor Pinhas Minkow-sky arrived from Odessa to take his place at the cantor's stand in the Eldridge Street Synagogue. The acquisition of Minkowsky was a coup for Kahal Adath Jeshurun: the congregation was competing with neighboring synagogues to draw crowds for the High Holiday services, and the immigrant population's enthusi-asm for cantors was such that a man of his stature could possibly trump the syna-gogue's architectural beauty as an attraction. Indeed, Minkowsky's presence in New York so thrilled the *Yidishe gazeten* that it delayed its review of the syna-gogue dedication until the day of his arrival: "The world-famous cantor Mr. Min-kowsky from Odessa arrived today and the congregation can be very proud of its beautiful, magnificent synagogue and the world-renowned cantor." Clearly, Kahal Adath Jeshurun was well positioned for the approaching High Holidays: the day after Minkowsky's arrival and the review in the *Yidishe gazeten*, the congregation sold $950 in tickets.[1]

Minkowsky's hiring must be seen in the context of the contemporary cantor craze. Lower East Side congregations combed eastern Europe for prospects in the quest to increase membership, transforming the position of cantor into a celebrity role. In the words of the rabbi Moses Weinberger: "A series of advertisements, letters, and telegrams flew from place to place across the Jewish world, creating a sensation among *chazanim* [cantors] everywhere. The enormous sums bandied about—$1,500, $2,000, $3,000—aroused excitement in every corner, and reached

Cantor's Stand

At the intricately carved cantor's stand the cantor faces east, toward Jerusalem. The ledge holds music sheets or prayer books, and sawtooth hinges adjust the ledge to the cantor's height. Photograph © 2007 by Kate Milford.

many receptive ears. The finest, most wonderful *chazanim* came over in large numbers." Credit for inciting the craze must be attributed to the Anshe Suwalk congregation, which in 1885, having bought and renovated a former church, imported Cantor Chaim Weinshel and paid him $1,000 a year. Soon thereafter, the Kalwarier Synagogue invited Cantor Israel Cooper to come to New York from Vilna. In the spring of 1886, Beth Hamedrash Hagadol brought Cantor Israel Michalovsky from Paris for the unprecedented sum of $4,000 a year.[2]

Given the level of competition, Kahal Adath Jeshurun might have prioritized the search for a cantor early on, but instead the congregation waited until August 1887, a mere month before the synagogue opened, to secure a big-name cantor. Having built the first synagogue in the neighborhood, the congregation perhaps reasoned that their architectural advantage would spare them the need for such an expense and that Cantor S. Jacobsohn, who had served them at the Allen Street Synagogue, would suffice. However, in the late summer of 1887, when rival congregations printed impressive advertisements featuring their celebrity cantors, Kahal Adath Jeshurun scrambled to secure a cantor of the first rank.[3]

Kahal Adath Jeshurun's appointment of Minkowsky created such excitement in the community that the cantor craze itself became associated with him, leading a usually meticulous chronicler of the Lower East Side, Judah David Eisenstein, to claim that Minkowsky himself had sparked the craze. In fact, he was the fourth great cantor to arrive in New York, his presence the result of a fad already well under way.[4]

The career of the Eldridge Street Synagogue's first cantor exemplifies the intermingling of commerce, religion, and music in the early immigrant community. Although the founders had constructed a house of worship for sacred activities, building and maintaining it involved them in business negotiations with architects, construction crews, and, most important, the East River Savings Bank, which held their $50,000 mortgage. Some wealthy members gave donations and guaranteed interest-free loans when needed, but the bulk of the expenses had to be covered by a steady and solvent membership. This is where music intertwines with commerce and religion. The east European immigrants had great affection for cantors and their music. Having a great cantor could attract members to a synagogue and could also induce nonmembers to buy tickets for special cantorial concerts. As the number of Jewish immigrants increased, congregations exchanged old rental halls and storefronts for lofty renovated church buildings or brand-new synagogues and engaged in the outreach needed to attract a paying membership and raise funds to support their new edifices. By hiring well-known cantors, congregational leaders sought to direct the crowds' love of music toward support of their religious institutions, and the desire to draw more and more crowds inspired the frenzied searches for the next cantorial sensation.[5]

The Eldridge Street Synagogue's leaders, not to be outdone by their neighbors, issued an invitation to Cantor Minkowsky in August 1887. Minkowsky, courted by established congregations in both Odessa and Vilna, had already created a stir in eastern Europe, but the New York invitation and the attention the American cantor craze had bestowed upon his profession piqued his interest. As he recalled in an autobiographical essay, "The Eldridge Street Synagogue was then the greatest and richest Orthodox synagogue in America; there were then in New York many distinguished and important cantors brought over, and the congregations competed with each other as to who was the best." Still, Minkowsky was not quite ready to leave Odessa, so he replied with a list of "very difficult" conditions that he imagined the American congregation would not be able to satisfy.[6]

To Minkowsky's surprise, in a return telegram his would-be employers not only agreed to his conditions but also promised the money needed to extricate him from his current contract. He could not resist the package, which included a five-year contract at $2,500 per annum, 1,000 rubles to release him from his current contract, first-class passage for himself and his family, $300 to set up a home in New York, and a six-week vacation every summer. Whereas many cantorial contracts obligated the cantor to pay for choirs out of his own pocket, Minkowsky's contract generously allowed the "congregation treasury" to cover the cost. The amount of money involved and the timing of the negotiations underscore the congregation's determination to hire Minkowsky; in August, a reporter speculated that the congregation had spent "hundreds of dollars" on cablegrams alone. The lucrative and accommodating contract set Minkowsky above competing cantors, not to mention the average New York City worker, whose earnings in 1880 totaled approximately $434.[7] Among those employed by Kahal Adath Jeshurun, the religious functionary earning the second-highest annual income, Leib Matlawsky,

Pinhas Minkowsky
    Cantor Minkowsky, who had a distinguished career in
Odessa, was in New York from 1887 to 1892 to serve as head
cantor at the Eldridge Street Synagogue, which he described as
the "greatest and richest Orthodox synagogue in America." From
Pinhas Minkowsky, "Otobiografye," in Jewish Ministers and
Cantors Association of America, *Di geshikhte fun khazones*
(New York: Pinski-Massel), 1924.

the longtime secretary and *bal koyre,* or Torah reader, earned a relatively paltry
$300.

While the contract specified his obligations as they pertained to the liturgi-
cal calendar, written between the lines was a desire for Minkowsky to project a
dual image: Orthodoxy and Americanization. The role of the cantor, the chazan,
was that of *sheliekh tsiber,* a messenger from the congregation to God, so it made
sense for the congregation to seek someone who could represent their position as
immigrants looking to both their collective past and their emergent future. As the
historian Jonathan Sarna explains: "The chazan was an ideal role model: observant yet rich, traditional yet modern. He formed a bridge between East Europe
and the East Side."[8] Minkowsky's biography was one that Lower East Side immigrants could relate to. Like them, he hailed from a small town in the Pale of Settlement—in this case, Beyala Tserkov in Ukraine. After studying with his father, the
town cantor, he had ventured beyond the Pale of Settlement to Vienna to study
music and secular subjects. After training, he served as cantor in Kherson, Lem-
berg (present-day L'viv), and Odessa, acquiring by his late twenties a professional
reputation and ambition that extended beyond his hometown. Like the worshippers on Eldridge Street, he had traveled, encountered urban life, and grasped the
importance of weaving innovation into tradition. Minkowsky enhanced the traditional Hebrew liturgy with his modern musical sensibility; he also used modern
research techniques to investigate and document the history of Jewish music.

Contemporary reports portrayed the hiring of Minkowsky as an "advertising scheme" designed to "achieve higher prices for pews and admission tickets."
Although the congregation may have disputed this characterization of its engage-

ment in the cantor craze, its own advertisement in the Yiddish papers the weekend before the synagogue's dedication on September 4, 1887, made explicit the link between the new cantor and the sale of seats: "The world-famous Cantor Pinhas Minkowsky, now cantor in Odessa . . . will arrive next week to take his position. This Monday you can come to the synagogue to buy or rent seats. Each person will be able to see for himself that a seat in this synagogue that is great, spacious, and airy, is worth what many men would pay. Our cantor Mr. Minkowsky from Odessa is without doubt the greatest in America . . . hurry to our synagogue to reserve your seats."[9] In this description the "spacious and airy" synagogue would merely serve as background to the cantor's performance. The sense of competition that stimulated the cantor craze also triumphs in these sentences, where Minkowsky is heralded not only as "world-famous" but also as "the greatest in America." Having entered the cantor craze in the last hour, Eldridge Street invested heavily in Minkowsky and now grasped the urgency with which they needed to call attention to his association with their congregation.

Once installed at the synagogue, Minkowsky helped his congregation retain essential elements of Orthodox custom while also embracing modern disciplines of study, as well as the modern art of pleasing the press. Eisenstein recalled that Minkowsky's habit of leading his choir with a pitch pipe in hand on the Sabbath and holidays alarmed the more traditional members, who feared that this practice violated Sabbath law. Although we do not know whether Minkowsky or the traditionalists prevailed, the historical record reveals that the controversy was resolved amicably and did not detract from his appeal. He drew both American and Yiddish journalists and photographers to the synagogue, and it no doubt pleased congregants to read about their cantor, dubbed "the Sweet Singer of Israel," in the New York newspapers. When uptown representatives from Reform congregations arrived to woo him to their platforms, Minkowsky maintained his loyalty to the Eldridge Street Synagogue and its Orthodox tradition. He also lent the congregation additional intellectual prestige by serving on the faculty of the Jewish Theological Seminary. His activities helped the congregation to "win" the cantor competition: as Minkowsky recalled in his autobiography, the congregation often boasted that "Minkowsky 'beat' all the other cantors."[10] In appreciation, the congregation granted him a $500 annual bonus for the first several years of his contract.

The granting of this bonus proved to be a thorny issue later, with the waning of the Lower East Side cantor craze. According to the synagogue minutes of December 1890, Minkowsky had sent a letter requesting his annual bonus. The congregation voted against it but the next month overwhelmingly resolved to offer him a bonus for the coming year; the account of the deliberations suggests that the congregation denied Minkowsky the bonus not because he displeased them but rather because they lacked the necessary funds. When the fall of 1891 rolled around, however, they could not make good on the past winter's intentions. The minute-book entry for November 15, 1891, reads: "Unanimously resolved that this year the congregation will give no gift because the treasury is in arrears."[11]

In response, Minkowsky wrote an emotional letter in which he both invoked the custom of a bonus and defended his professionalism: "Sirs: I am sincerely hurt, since until now I was treated with a great deal of respect, and I, for my part, executed my position with loyalty and dignity. And at the end, this relationship is being damaged by this bitter and regrettable conflict. Just because you have overestimated your budget and created castles in the air, it is not my fault. You have shattered me for no good reason and you have hurt my pride." Minkowsky was justified in accusing the congregation of overestimating its income; it could be argued that a more budget-conscious congregation never would have erected a synagogue that carried a price tag of close to $100,000. But as the congregation tightened its belt and struggled to gain control of its finances in the early 1890s, the leaders found it easier to eliminate the cantor's bonus than to sell the building. They may even have reconsidered the sizable monthly payments due to Minkowsky as part of the contract; according to Eisenstein, the "congregation decided that it was too difficult to pay such a huge salary."[12]

Both the congregation's minutes and its bank books support the lack of finances as the reason for their refusal to grant the bonus, yet Minkowsky's correspondence suggests that more than money was at stake. The minutes indicate a congregation in increasingly straitened financial circumstances. In early 1892 the leaders decided to review Minkowsky's contract and officially transcribe it into the minutes. This may have been done to verify that the contract did not specify a bonus but also to check the terms of the contract as the five-year term wound to a close. Meanwhile, Minkowsky's dissatisfaction grew, and in May 1892 he resigned: "A note was received from the cantor. He declares that we spare ourselves the trouble of debating about him because he has been called back to Odessa. He demands that he be given a gift of $500. He will travel back two months before the expiration of his contract."[13] This item in the minutes supports the notion that the congregation had debated whether to renew Minkowsky's contract and confirms that Minkowsky had not forgiven the congregation's failure to grant the bonus.

Thirty years later, in an autobiographical essay, Minkowsky made no mention of the bonus and suggested that his decision to accept an invitation from the Brody Synagogue in Odessa had more to do with respect and honor than with money. Despite his love for America, "the luckiest country," and New York, "the greatest city," he extolled the "ideal and humane treatment" with which the Brody Synagogue treated its religious functionaries: "They celebrate 50-year anniversaries of their choir members, sextons—and of cantors you don't even need to talk. Christian janitors are there for four generations, you pass your position to your son, grandson, and then to your great-grandson. The personnel from an institution are treated as family, not as ordinary employees."[14] Although Minkowsky never directly slighted the Eldridge Street Synagogue, by invoking the Odessa congregation's treatment of its personnel as his motivation for leaving New York, he was presumably pointing to the corresponding lack at the American synagogue. Indeed, we see here the same desire for respect that he registered in his 1891 letter to the congregation requesting his bonus. Had he merely been interested in a higher salary, he could have remained in New York, for Rabbi Bernard Drachman's new Zichron Ephraim Synagogue, on Park Avenue and East Sixty-seventh Street, had also offered him a position.

By 1892 the cantor craze had apparently waned, with consequences for the ways major congregations sought and selected their new cantors. Congregations no longer believed that allocating a significant proportion of their expenses for the salaries of star cantors was worthwhile. Also, a new crop of would-be cantors had arrived in the United States. Although they lacked the stature of Minkowsky, Cooper, Michalovsky, and Weinshel, their salaries were a fraction of the cost. By this time, the Kalwarier shul had dismissed Cooper, and a dissatisfied Weinshel had left the Anshe Suwalk congregation. Rather than comb Europe for replacements, the major congregations held auditions. The substitution of American-style auditions, in which prospective candidates were judged solely on performance, not training, created a context very different from the earlier one. In the mid-1880s congregations relied on east European communal leaders for advice when hiring. In 1891, Weinshel mockingly underscored this shift by telling of a former miller who won the auditions for a particular congregation. When the miller-turned-cantor wrote to his wife, still in Russia, of his new career, "the poor woman went into shock," believing that her husband had gone mad. Though perhaps exaggerated, this account, as ethnomusicologist Mark Slobin has shown, demonstrates how the Lower East Side search for European star cantors had abruptly ended.[15]

After Minkowsky's departure in July 1892, the congregation laid out their new process for finding a cantor and the criteria for selecting him: "It was resolved to advertise in the newspaper that the synagogue is ready to hold auditions for cantors. No specific price should be set. The congregation will set it according to the quality of the applicants. Above all, a cantor should be capable of conducting prayer services himself, know the rules of music, and also should be able to pray with a choir. No remuneration will be given for auditions." Rather than comb Europe for the best talent, they decided to look locally. The decision to offer no remuneration for auditions reflects the abundance of potential cantors in the neighborhoods. Several rounds of auditions yielded Yehezkel Borenstain, who was hired only for the High Holiday season and given a total of $500, from which he was expected to hire a choir. Apparently, Borenstain did not satisfy the congregation, for he failed to garner the two-thirds majority vote needed to grant him a year's contract.[16] For several years, the congregation contented itself with hiring cantors on a monthly basis—at $30 a month as opposed to the $208.50 Minkowsky had received. But the parade of cantors displeased the congregation, and the leadership ultimately decided to once again hire a permanent cantor. These cantors, however, earned only $500 or $600 for the year. Not until the 1910s did the cantor's yearly salary reach $1,000—still not approaching Minkowsky's pay or, presumably, status.

This change in employment practices illustrates a dramatic shift in power from the cantor to the lay leaders. In 1887, Minkowsky had set his own terms. But the market had changed considerably in the past five years, and the lay leadership — president, treasurer, and trustees — saw no need to commit to an exorbitant yearly salary to attract a well-known cantor when the congregation could still satisfy the desire for name recognition and could still entice the ticket-buying public by hiring a visiting cantor for a one-performance weekend. By 1913, the congregation could afford a cantor, Pinhas Novakovsky, whom they would hail as "world-renowned" in their promotion of a holiday concert.[17]

The power of the laity and the disempowerment of religious functionaries were in no way unique to the Eldridge Street Synagogue; rather, they were indicative of broader trends on the Lower East Side. The Yiddish press argued that the immigrant community was in a state of *hefker*, or anarchy, with multitudes of congregations, lodges, and schools all struggling to gain control of their own affairs and paying no attention to overall community welfare. Secular studies replaced religious studies, and ascending the capitalist ladder became increasingly important. It was in this context that the well-being of cantors, rabbis, and scholars was overlooked, and the religious functionaries lost both earning power and respect. In 1908, Jacob Pfeffer of the *Morgn zhurnal* noted that a rabbi was "paid less than a common pants-operator or an errand boy. . . . It is simply a scandal. The entire community uses the rabbi, to whom they go to ask a question, and there are enough who ask questions, but no one asks the question, how does the rabbi make a living? Does the rabbi not have a mouth, and don't his children need to eat, and doesn't his landlord require rent?" Pfeffer acknowledged that rabbis and cantors were not amply compensated in Europe but countered that in Europe, at least, they had "respect and recognition." To remedy the situation, Pfeffer encouraged the community to organize and recommended that a rabbi from Europe be brought over to provide motivation and leadership. Rabbis, not businessmen, should lead the immigrant Jews; he encouraged "Jews who have God and Jewishness in their hearts [to] do their best to drive from the synagogues the low element that pulls all the strings with the checkbook instead of the Torah."[18]

When we apply Pfeffer's analysis to the Eldridge Street Synagogue, we see that although his depiction of the lay leaders as coarse, money-driven ignoramuses is off the mark, he speaks to a larger truth: a communal shift in focus from scholarship to business. The leaders at Eldridge Street possessed a sound and active knowledge of Jewish texts and spearheaded Jewish communal endeavors. And while they certainly controlled the purse strings, that control entailed taking responsibility for the congregation's bills and mortgage payments. In 1887 investing heavily in a star cantor had been cost effective, but by 1892, cantors who were able to perform well in auditions sufficed. Having taken the lead from other congregations in the mid-1880s who started the trend of importing star cantors, Kahal Adath Jeshurun's leadership now took a cue from the same congregations, who were content with local talent. If the competing congregations hired locally at local rates and still attracted crowds, why should Kahal Adath Jeshurun alone commit to expensive cantorial contracts?

This background also helps us understand why Minkowsky, a scholar as well as a cantor, preferred Odessa to New York. In Europe he could find the support, respect, and, perhaps most important, the intellectual camaraderie to sustain him. A good deal of his prestige came from his scholarship, not just his trained tenor voice. As a theorist and a historian of Jewish music, Minkowsky wrote articles for the Hebrew, Yiddish, German, and Russian press in Europe. Upon his return to Odessa, he flourished in the nurturing environment of a congregation that valued him, and formed a fruitful collaboration with the Brody Synagogue's composer and choirmaster, David Novakowsky. Throughout his tenure at the Brody Synagogue, whose services attracted visitors of all religions and backgrounds, Minkowsky published many compositions and theoretical and historical articles about Jewish music. If he had found a community in New York where he could be appreciated, in Odessa he had colleagues like Chaim Bialik, Sholem Aleichem, and Mendele Mokher Sforim, who not only provided intellectual stimulation but touted Minkowsky's importance and even discussed his career in their work. He remained at the Brody Synagogue for thirty years, finally leaving when the Soviet regime made life uncomfortable for the Jewish community.[19]

The complicated politics of respect, money, and power notwithstanding, the immigrant population continued to demand Jewish music and cantors. Understandably, a population caught in the throes of adaptation—seeking employment, working seven-day weeks, supporting children in America and often parents still in Europe—did not have the means to join a synagogue, much less to scrutinize

Ticket to Cantorial Concert
    Cantorial performances remained an important element of Eldridge Street Synagogue services well into the twentieth century. The green ticket from 1913 promises a festive Hanukah concert with the congregation's "beloved world-famous" Cantor Pinhas Novakovsky taking a starring role.

a cantor's scholarly credentials or to analyze the priorities of synagogue leadership. Yet when the High Holidays came around, many found the synagogue services hard to resist. Advertisements announcing "famous" cantors filled the Yiddish newspapers, and congregations plastered "posters, playbills, advertisements, handbills, circulars and announcements" all over their facades, "from the roof to the basement." Like the newspaper advertisements, flyers played up the cantor: in one a cantor's voice was hailed as "five hundred times stronger and sweeter than Caruso's"; it had the power to "'render obscure all the other singers and cantors from the time of the six days of creation up to the present.'"[20] Such advertisements suggest a strong interest in the High Holiday services and the cantor from those outside the immediate synagogue membership; members would have been able to learn of the upcoming cantor at services. Indeed, people who did not attend synagogue regularly lined up for the High Holiday services, as Ida Rothman Feely recalled. Although her father worked seven days a week and thus could not attend synagogue regularly, "he enjoyed listening to the cantors who chanted songs from the Bible and would attend the Synagogue on the High Holidays if a well known cantor was going to participate in the service."[21]

    As part of an effort to cultivate reader participation and loyalty, the *Forverts*, or *Jewish Daily Forward*, solicited "stories about cantors" in September 1902: "Now is the time to send us true stories about them. Jews are a musical people and their folk spirit in this respect expresses itself chiefly in the songs of cantors and choir boys. For Jews there are no more interesting stories than stories about cantors." For a socialist newspaper to select cantors as its September topic, right before the High Holidays, speaks volumes about the profound enthusiasm for cantors and their music shared by the immigrant generation. As Slobin confirms, "It

Advertisement for Cantorial Concert
By the 1930s the congregation could no longer afford
yearlong cantors but made sure to hire cantors for the High Holiday
season. This 1948 advertisement in the *Morgn zhurnal-tageblat*
highlights the young cantor Max Fuchs.

is difficult to overrate the social importance of the cantor for the musical culture"
at that time. The cantor continued to be associated with the synagogue — even the
sheet music published by the Hebrew Publishing Company featured photographs
of cantors set into drawings of synagogues. At the same time, the appeal of the
cantor began to transcend the synagogue; workers could find stories about them
in their newspapers, and the growing availability of sheet music and, later, recordings shows that the cantor appealed to people beyond the synagogue walls. In
1933 a *Forverts* writer still puzzled over "why cantorial music is so popular among
the wide Jewish masses, even those who are entirely far from religious traditional
life."[22]

Throughout the period of immigrant adaptation, then, the cantor remained a
crucial figure, but what was required of him changed in a way that made a cantor
of Minkowsky's stature less likely to find a permanent position. The Americaniza-

tion of the cantor role resulted in a greater social emphasis being placed on performance than background and training. In addition, new media made it possible for people to enjoy cantorial music with phonographs and sheet music, which eventually detracted from the individual cantor's ability to support himself through a professional role in a congregation. These trends were observed on both sides of the Atlantic. Minkowsky himself later strongly disapproved of the availability of cantorial music through recordings in Odessa, "citing reports that one could hear sacred hymns coming out of the rooms of prostitutes in the city's pleasure quarters."[23]

Minkowsky returned to the United States in 1922, where he served as honorary president of the Cantors' Association. By this time, he found it difficult to secure a permanent cantorial position and traveled to various cities to lead special services. He died before long, at the age of sixty-five, on January 18, 1924, and the *New York Times* as well as the Yiddish papers published obituaries. The *Tageblat*, in particular, noted Minkowsky's contribution to Jewish musical scholarship, calling him a fine "Hebrew stylist" whose cantorial career and scholarship proved that "he was a fighter for the noble Jewish music, and the purity of synagogue music."[24]

At the funeral procession and at the memorial services that took place in Boston, Philadelphia, and New York, prominent rabbis, cantors, and journalists gathered to eulogize Minkowsky, and cantors and choirs chanted the appropriate mourning prayers to the hundreds in attendance. As the *New York Times* reported, despite severe winter weather that "kept many streets of the city deserted all day," more than a thousand people attended Minkowsky's funeral service on the Lower East Side, with Cantor Joseph Rosenblatt conducting two hundred cantors and one hundred choir singers, making the service "one of the most impressive ever on the east side." In paying tribute to Minkowsky, Jewish immigrants once again demonstrated the centrality of Jewish music in their lives, confirming the *Tageblat*'s declaration that "Minkowsky's death is a great loss for Jewish music in particular, and for the Jewish people in general."[25]

Without a doubt, Minkowsky's arrival in 1887 helped solidify Kahal Adath Jeshurun's reputation as a major congregation on the Lower East Side, attracting both new members and visitors to the synagogue. Although money outweighed music in the end and although Minkowsky stayed at the Eldridge Street Synagogue for less than five years, what he represented—a balance between Orthodoxy and modernism, tradition and innovation—persisted at the Eldridge Street Synagogue during its prime. The comfort that cantorial music provided to immigrants across the ideological and religious spectrum remained a constant. When Minkowsky returned to America, a fellow cantor praised his delivery as "genuinely Jewish and yet modern."[26] His ability to straddle these worlds made him a hero, a sheliekh tsiber, to the east European Jewish community in the United States.

FIVE

E Pluribus Unum

O N A SATURDAY MORNING in May 1902, two women rushed into the synagogue's sanctuary in the midst of Sabbath prayer services. Their entrance to the male-occupied floor no doubt turned heads. The next steps they took, ascending the bimah, in the center of the sanctuary, must have attracted the attention of the entire congregation, including those seated in the women's balcony. This was their intention. The women had come to protest what they believed to be a grave infraction of social justice, and according to tradition, matters of social justice allowed for an interruption in the Torah services. On this occasion, the price of kosher meat in New York had risen from twelve to eighteen cents a pound, rendering it unaffordable for the majority of the immigrant families. The immigrant women, the primary household shoppers, were leading a remarkably successful effort to boycott the meat. As the historian Paula Hyman has shown, these women applied their knowledge of American labor techniques and vocabulary to uphold the Jewish dietary laws, kashruth. The protests, including mass meetings and attacks on butcher shops, had already grabbed front-page headlines in the major New York City newspapers, not to mention the Yiddish dailies.[1]

Saturday, the Jewish Sabbath, required different tactics. That morning, groups of women had dispersed to synagogues large and small to plead the case for a boycott on kosher meat. At the Eldridge Street Synagogue, the pair ascended to the bimah and asked the congregation to officially support the boycott. Aaron Kommel, president of the congregation, assured the women that they would be

Bimah

The bimah, or reading platform, is in the center of the sanctuary. During the Torah reading, worshippers in the least expensive seats, at the rear of the sanctuary, could hear the chanting just as well as the leaders seated in the expensive seats at the front. Photograph © 2007 by Kate Milford.

discussing the matter the next day at their congregational meeting. Either Kommel felt that the prayer service was not the proper venue for such a matter, or he sensed the potential divisiveness of the issue. In any case, "the women did not budge." According to the account in the *Forverts,* the younger of the two delivered a "fiery speech," directed particularly to the women in the balcony, urging a *kheyrem,* or boycott, of kosher meat. Kommel tried again to lead them off the reading platform, "but the women were not silenced." At this point, Isaac Gellis, a leading manufacturer of kosher sausages and consequently no fan of the boycott, apparently gestured to his friend David Cohen, a former congregation president like himself. Cohen, described in the *Forverts* as a "real estatenik," ascended the bimah. He acknowledged the exorbitant price of kosher meat and the justness of the women's cause but then explained that the congregation could not endorse a boycott because, he feared, the boycott would force the community to purchase and consume non-kosher meat. It was better to buy half the amount of meat needed, Cohen advised, attempting to placate both the women and his friend Gellis. A commotion broke out: "There was a tumult. From all sides people yelled, 'No meat! No meat!'" The "frightened" Cohen left the bimah, and the women presumably continued to the next synagogue.[2] The Yiddish papers the next day reported that the majority of congregations warmly received the women, and within a few weeks the boycott had succeeded in bringing the price of kosher meat down to fourteen cents.

Much contemporary commentary portrayed synagogue goers as "bent graybearded old Jews," who built their synagogues as refuges from America. This incident, however, establishes that the synagogue was a place to debate current events and, further, that religious matters were themselves current events.[3] When the "agitators" voiced concern over the price of kosher meat, they directed their message to the balcony, where the women, those who held consumer power, prayed. The congregational leadership responded with an eye toward appeasing a shop-owning member, but the vociferous reaction of the congregants tells its own tale: the synagogue offered space for dissension.

The interruption — which probably lasted only a few minutes and after which the congregation certainly resumed the prayer services — shows how American politics, culture, and mores affected the workings of synagogues. While dramatic incidents were not the norm, the members of the Eldridge Street Synagogue were constantly engaged with their surroundings. Visiting on a more serene Saturday, the journalist Richard Wheatley pronounced the congregation "an impressive representation of traditional Judaism, modified perforce by the spirit of the time and surroundings."[4] Rituals, customs, fasts, feasts, prayer, and festivals celebrated there were not mere vestiges of east European tradition transplanted by unwitting devotees but the products of an active and intriguing adaptation to American life. This particular incident highlights certain dynamics of the adaptation: the diversity of the congregation, the complex role of women in religious life, and questions about the conduct and decorum of the synagogue service itself. Focusing on three architectural elements—grooves in the floor, the women's balcony, and the bimah—allows us to explore these themes in the heyday of the synagogue, from 1890 to 1915.

Wheatley perceived the very diversity of worshippers at Eldridge Street to be integral to the congregation's ability to adapt to America: "Lawyers, merchants, artisans, clerks, peddlers, and laborers compose the dense and changeful throng. All are one in respect to race and faith, but many in regard to birthplace and speech. *E pluribus Unum* receives a new meaning here." The throng of worshippers came from the various economic, religious, and geographical backgrounds represented by the neighborhood's Jewish residents. Uniting for prayer, this diverse congregation left a physical imprint on the sanctuary that serves as an evocative visual corollary to the American motto. Today, a century after Wheatley wrote, horizontal grooves undulate throughout the sanctuary floor, worn into the pine boards by the thousands of worshippers who stood there shifting their feet. The grooves are the result of the shifting forward and backward of feet in prayer, called *shokeling* in Yiddish. Wheatley observed the congregants at prayer and poetically described the group as "ceaseless in gentle movements."[5] Over time, the feet of immigrants young and old, from countless hometowns, and of varied professions wore grooves in the sanctuary floorboards, preserved to this day.

Kahal Adath Jeshurun, the People's Congregation of the Just, adopted an inclusive name and cultivated members who came from all over eastern Europe, in particular the broad swath of cities in the eastern parts of Congress Poland and of Lithuania. This inclusiveness was atypical; by the 1880s and 1890s most congre-

Grooves in the Floor
    The shuffling feet of thousands of worshippers made grooves in
the sanctuary floor. The restorers decided to preserve the grooves to show
the congregation's interaction with the building over time. Photograph
© 2006 by Kate Milford.

gations forming on the Lower East Side were associated with particular regions or
towns in eastern Europe: Anshe Suwalk, the People of Suwalk; Anshe Kalwarier,
the People of Kalwarier; Anshe Bialystock, the People of Bialystock.[6]

The cosmopolitan nature of the Eldridge Street congregation was from the
start a function of practicality, first for Beth Hamedrash and later for Kahal Adath
Jeshurun. In the early years, it enabled them to form an east European congrega-

tion, and in the pivotal years of the late 1880s and early 1890s, as they built and dedicated their new synagogue and organized their congregation, it enabled them to embrace the number of immigrants needed to fill their seats. In 1852, we know that the pioneering men of Beth Hamedrash — who also gave their congregation a universal name, meaning "House of Study" — welcomed men of Russian and Polish extraction to fill the quorum for prayer. Indeed, it was not until the 1870s and 1880s, when the east European Jewish migration increased in scale, that east European immigrants had the luxury of forming congregations based on a shared hometown identity. One of these, Holkhe Yosher Vizaner (Those Who Walk in Righteousness), whose members came from Vizan, formed in 1870 and dropped its name and particular allegiance to Vizan in 1886 to merge with Beth Hamedrash. The merged congregation adopted the inclusive name of Kahal Adath Jeshurun and focused on attracting as many members as possible to their "magnificent synagogue on the three lots of 12-14-16 Eldridge," opening the doors to anyone comfortable with the rites as practiced in "Poland and Lithuania."[7]

The historian Jeffrey Gurock has referred to Eldridge Street's congregation as "proto-Americanized" precisely because it subscribed to a vision of Jewry that moved beyond hometown loyalties to embrace an American standard of decorum and architecture. A handsome building, a large and diverse congregation, a fashionable cantor, a dignified service: these components became the norm for American Jews of east European descent by the 1920s. Having achieved this forty years earlier, Kahal Adath Jeshurun attracted bankers and peddlers, lawyers and clerks, who liked the idea of an Orthodox identity attuned to the geography and customs of America. Even into the 1920s, some congregants held two memberships, one at a local or hometown association, which they maintained out of obligation to a parent, and one at the Eldridge Street Synagogue, which they personally preferred. Naomi Groob Fuchs's father, Morris, who held office at the synagogue from the 1920s into the 1950s, also belonged to the small synagogue on Henry Street, which his father had attended: "You see, everybody had more than one shul."[8]

Although the Eldridge Street Synagogue has been called downtown's "first rich man's congregation," the vast majority of the grooves in the floor must have been made by less affluent people. The congregation's constitutions, ledgers, and seat records substantiate a social mix in membership. Some members certainly made initial deposits in the hundreds of dollars and paid annual dues in this range, but many paid closer to $30 a year. It was even possible to rent a seat for $10 and pay in quarterly installments of $2.50. In comparison, tickets to the Yiddish theater, which many immigrants attended on a weekly basis, cost up to $1.00 a show. Richard Wheatley noted mingling of artisans, clerks, peddlers, and laborers with merchants and lawyers. Since, with the exception of certain holiday services, which required tickets, the congregation opened its prayer services to the public, drop-ins who had no formal affiliation with the synagogue might have added to the occupational and economic diversity.[9]

Special offers and procedures were designed to win new members and retain current ones. In February 1887, Isidor Abrahams purchased seat 1 for $1,100. He was surely the most generous and wealthy member of his day: the following September he also donated $1,600 for the ark and the bimah, and in the Rosh Hashanah season of 1889 he underwrote the two side arks, which housed the scrolls of the Prophets. Yet even Abrahams paid only 25 percent of the list price for his seat, and ten years later he still owed $500. Another eastern-wall seatholder, David Cohen, pledged $875 for seat 10 but paid just $50, or less than 6 percent of the list price. Away from the ark, the price of the rows decreased, and most seats carried a list price in the $250 range, which on average took in 25 percent of the list price. If the list prices were shockingly expensive, the actual financing of seat purchase was much more gradual and affordable, with many congregants making initial deposits and paying only interest in subsequent years. Within a decade, men of more moderate means than Abrahams and Cohen dominated the congregation, but they also benefited from gradual payment plans, making from three to nine payments a year. In 1897–1898 only 4 members out of 150 paid sums of more than $100, while 80 percent paid less than $40 a year, 49 percent paid less than $30, and 22 percent paid less than $20. In March 1898, "it was advertised in the newspapers that members would be admitted free, without an entrance fee." By 1913 the cost of renting a seat had decreased to $8.[10]

Whether renting or holding a seat, members of the Eldridge Street Synagogue gained not only a place to worship but also access to a community that offered essential educational, financial, and medical support. Even seat rental entitled a member to a range of benefits, including the right to attend general meetings and vote on all congregational issues, with the exception of matters relating to the building itself, such as whether to install electricity or paint the sanctuary.[11] It presented them with the opportunity to use the synagogue's collection of scholarly books, attend coordinated study sessions, and form a community through study. Benefits also included a seat for a member's wife (except for widows, in the early days all members were men), access to doctors hired by the congregation, funeral rites, and payments to a member's widow and family after the member's death. If a close relative of a member died, obligating him to sit shivah, to mourn for the traditional seven days, the congregation alleviated the financial burden resulting from missed work by paying the member $5 in *shivah gelt*. The congregation also coordinated visits to sick members and often held collections to benefit a member in financial trouble. Creative means were sometimes employed to raise money. When Lipman Harris fell ill, for example, rather than just pooling the community's resources, the committee assigned to assist Harris's "very needy situation" proposed "to buy a diamond ring and raffle it off for the benefit of the sick brother."[12]

Although membership benefits were accorded to both renters and seatholders, for the first twenty-five years Kahal Adath Jeshurun was established, only seatholders could hold the major offices of president, vice president, and treasurer. In the first ten years, the presidency rotated among the elite—Sender Jarmulowsky, David Cohen, Isaac Gellis, and Nathan Hutkoff—leaving the nonelite and the renters to content themselves with trustee positions and leading to much debate.[13] In a congregation that had established a democratic means of functioning, complete with a constitution with bylaws and articles governing membership, elections, and the nomination process, the reign of a prominent and wealthy but slim minority did not last.

Renters had aspired to and were even elected to leadership positions, thereby prompting a rule clarification in 1892, when it was requested that the seatholding requirement be specified in the minutes. Again in 1901 the distinction seems to have been either temporarily forgotten or ignored, for a November election brought Moshe Ziskind Feinsilber, a renter, to the position of vice president, prompting the objection of a former president: "Brother David Cohen introduced a written protest that he, Feinsilber, was illegally nominated and illegally elected, because according to our by-law in the Minute Book, p. 161, members who do not own their seats but only rent them, cannot be nominated for the office of president, vice president or treasurer. There was much debate about this. Mr. Feinsilber re-signed." At this point the newly elected treasurer, Shmuel Richman, resigned be-cause that he did not own his seat either.[14] The 1901 election debacle reaffirmed the seatholders' claim to leadership, but it also shows the congregation's changing views on leadership. Until a formal objection was raised, the congregation had nominated and elected renters for two out of the three major leadership positions. Cohen's protest prompted much debate, the discussion continued in subsequent years, and in 1913 a new constitution dropped seat ownership as a prerequisite for office.

From the beginning, recruitment efforts were aimed largely at young men, in part because of the medical and funeral expenses that older members would be more likely to incur. Men past the age of fifty constituted a separate category of membership, and they were charged more upon entrance: "The members have a right to set a higher price for an older candidate."[15] On the other hand, when a long-standing member reached the age of sixty and could no longer pay dues, he qualified as an "honorable member," which entitled him to keep a seat and all benefits for free. A younger membership and family loyalty were further encour-aged by the automatic acceptance of members' sons as members.

Although American currents of thought influenced the congregation to amend the leadership qualifications required by its constitution, the congregation withstood economic and social pressures to abandon observance of the Sabbath as a prerequisite for membership. The first requirement listed for membership, that "persons known to publicly violate the Sabbath, can not be admitted to member-ship" was reiterated several times in the constitution. In addition, officers of the synagogue could "not be guilty of violating the Sabbath laws," and members of the burial society had to be "strict observers" of the Sabbath.[16] This adherence to Sabbath observance was in keeping with the Orthodox tradition the congregation aimed to maintain regardless of economic and social circumstances. In eastern Europe employment conditions had enabled most Jews to observe the Sabbath be-cause they held jobs within Jewish economic sectors. A congregation there could depend on not only official community support but also freedom to attend services on Saturday given the workweek's pause for them to do so. In New York, however, the six-day workweek encompassed Saturday and even glorified it by making it payday. Orthodox congregations like the one at Eldridge Street, in upholding tradition and the importance of Sabbath observance, were standing against the cultural and economic tide.

During the High Holidays, Sabbath observers and Sabbath desecrators prayed together at Orthodox synagogues. Saturday workers clamored to attend services, and congregational leaders sold special holiday tickets. Visitors to the Eldridge Street Synagogue during the High Holidays would have noted the policemen on horseback shepherding the crowds of worshippers through the four doors and, once inside, the lack of seating for the worshippers, who overflowed into the aisles. One congregant, Yossi Paston, recalled the "packed shul" at turn-of-the-century holiday services. He said that the congregation even built extra seats to augment the 740 already in place. In 1906 the congregation hired prayer leaders and sold tickets to an additional 200 people, who filled the *bes medresh*, or street-level chapel and study hall, and in other years, it rented out the bes medresh to a lodge or congregation that arranged its own services.[17] Together, Sabbath-observant and non–Sabbath-observant worshippers welcomed the new Jewish year, atoned for their sins, and formed the essential communities for prayer mandated by the High Holidays.

As contemporary Yiddish and English newspapers reported, the ten-day period from Rosh Hashanah, the Jewish new year, to Yom Kippur, the Day of Atonement, was the season "when everybody goes" to synagogue. Even if—or precisely because—they had not attended synagogue the rest of the year, Jews often found that participating in public worship on the Days of Awe was essential. The American newspapers described how the worship services had the power to attract everyone from newly arrived adult immigrants to fully Americanized children. The surge in seekers of synagogue seats overwhelmed the synagogues in the immigrant neighborhoods, and temporary synagogues, or "mushroom synagogues," sprouted in movie theaters, halls, and even churches as entrepreneurs rented spaces, hired cantors, and sold tickets. The "season of piety" spurred established congregations to advertise their synagogues, promote their cantors, and sell

High Holiday Tickets
   Although most of the year worshippers could simply enter the sanctuary, during the High Holidays both members and nonmembers required tickets.

tickets to capitalize on the demand for services. According to the *New York Post*, "the net proceeds from the sale of seats are in many instances the main source of the congregation's income."[18]

   In 1909 the sale of High Holiday tickets provided 73 percent of the Eldridge Street Synagogue's annual income. A special seat committee composed of the most active and honored members formed in early August to allow between six and eight weeks for the sale, rental, and assignment of seats. The seat committee made arrangements "to have tickets printed for seats to be rented and also to have slips printed and to take care of these matters in the most fitting manner." The synagogue catered not only to those who prayed daily or weekly but also to those the Yiddish press referred to as "Yom Kippur Yiden," or Yom Kippur Jews. This outreach united immigrant Jews of varying religious customs and levels of observance, encompassing a wide spectrum of religious behavior. Many immigrants either could not or did not go to services regularly but sustained a relationship with a synagogue to mark holidays and rites of passage.[19] Over time, the tens of thousands who worshipped at the Eldridge Street Synagogue and slowly wore grooves in the sanctuary floor far exceeded the numbers listed on seatholder and membership rosters and deepened the meaning of *E pluribus unum*.

Whether attending on a Sabbath or a High Holiday, women entered the Eldridge Street Synagogue through the two doors located on the far northern and southern sides of the building. Their husbands, sons, brothers, and fathers entered through center doors leading to a small vestibule with immediate access to the sanctuary, but the women's path took them to twin staircases that spiraled up to the balcony. The open design of the three-sided balcony and the ways it was modified in the early years tells us much about the congregation's desire to hew to Orthodox tradition while also adopting "the spirit of the time and the surroundings."

According to Orthodox tradition, men and women sit separately during synagogue services. In America, however, the development of Reform Judaism prompted most synagogues to offer "family," or mixed seating, by 1880. Whether from cosmopolitan cities like Odessa or small provincial towns like Lubz, the east European immigrants at Eldridge Street, accustomed to houses of prayer that had maintained this division, strove to re-create what they considered the proper conditions for worship. The Eldridge Street Synagogue's seat contract for 1887 assured prospective seat owners of the following arrangement: "As it is the intention of all persons connected with said congregation to preserve, maintain and adhere to the strict Orthodox faith, it is hereby agreed, that, if at any time an organ should be used in connection with the service, if males and females are allowed to sit together during divine services; or if a mixed choir (males and females) is allowed to sing during divine services, the said [seat-owner] shall have the right to recover from the said congregation, twice the amount which he may have paid to said congregation from the dates of these presents, exclusive of interest and dues."[20] This clause and the architectural form it took—the women's balcony—provided not just a physical separation of the sexes but a rigid conceptual dividing line between Reform and Orthodox Judaism.

Still, there were adaptations, as indicated by a journalist's description of Rabbi Bernard Drachman at the synagogue's dedication: "His looks rested with a certain sort of satisfaction on the women's gallery, and his face beamed as he perceived that not one high hat was to be seen there, that in the congregation Kahal Adat Jeshurun there was a perfect women's section, which kept the sexes separated."[21] In other words, like many American synagogues, the Eldridge Street Synagogue had an open gallery that enabled men to look up and women to look down. In European synagogues, the separation of the sexes typically positioned women behind curtains, grilles, or, in much older synagogues, walls.

The view offered to the east European immigrant women from Eldridge's open balcony was in many ways an American development. As immigrant communities in the eighteenth and nineteenth centuries built their synagogues, they took their cues both from American houses of worship and from late-seventeenth-century and early eighteenth-century synagogues in Amsterdam and London. The historian Karla Goldman explains that interaction with Christian neighbors meant that as early as 1744, New York's first congregation, Shearith Israel, received visitors, and many of these visitors were critical of the policy of physical separation of the sexes. By the late eighteenth century, American houses of worship were mostly offering family worship, and the synagogue arrangements of the Jews stood out as unusual. Balconies, then, already used in western Europe, provided a compromise: men and women were separated but shared the worship space. Still, debate ensued over how high the balcony wall should be and whether congregations should supplement the separation with grillwork. When the Orthodox congregation Shearith Israel built a balcony in their first house of worship in 1730, they installed "breast-work as high as [the women's] chins," but by 1763 the Touro synagogue in Newport had experimented with an open gallery. Touro's open gallery proved influential, and when Shearith Israel built their second synagogue in 1818, the congregants also opted for an open instead of a "close front Gallery."[22]

The east European Jews who built the Eldridge Street Synagogue adopted the open gallery, yet like Shearith Israel seventy years earlier, expressed some am-

Women's Balcony
Women attended services in the balcony. Photograph © 2007 by Kate Milford.

bivalence about the design. Although they had commissioned the open three-sided balcony, or at least had failed to prevent the Herter Brothers from designing and building one, some hesitant voices must have argued for a more traditional separation, so curtains were added. This compromise did not sit well with the women. A mere four years after the opening, Richard Wheatley observed that "pierced curtains sliding on brass rods, like the ancient lattices in the British House of Commons, which permit the ladies to see without being seen, are supposed to seclude Hebrew femininity from the disturbing gaze of the masculinity. But they do not, for the simple reason that deft hands draw them aside, or throw them up, and vision is only supposedly obstructed. The old custom is not in favor with the majority, and will never be more popular, if it ever was, with them."[23]

Once the curtains were drawn by the women, the sloping floor of the balcony allowed those in the back rows as fine a view as those in the front. Miriam Aaron attended services in the 1920s and recalled how the banister "seemed to glow. Perhaps from the many years of gloved and ungloved hands moving along the banister's surface. I would stand next to my mother seated with the open prayer book in her lap, dressed in her best clothes, lean on the railing and look down on the assemblage of men and boys, heads covered by prayer shawls, chanting, mumbling, dozing, chatting with an adjacent worshipper. On occasion my father would glance up, shrug his shoulders, and smile. My parents always sat in their same respective seats."[24] The balcony was a core part of the sanctuary, with its own rules, assigned seating, and prayer books, and although the women were separated from the men, it allowed immediate and unobstructed access to the activity on the sanctuary floor.

On the balcony, women and girls quietly recited their prayers. In Gussie Dubrin's description, although the balcony was crowded, it was "very quiet" during services. Of course, the balcony, like the sanctuary below, was most crowded on Sabbaths and holidays, when children had to stand in the back to make room for the women. Rose Eisenberg recalled how in the late 1910s and 1920s women in the balcony listened in rapt attention to Rabbi Avrohom Aharon Yudelovitch's hour-long sermons, which "always made the women cry." Lillian Fried remembered that "as girls, we'd come and pat my mother on the shoulder, give her a kiss and then, if we got noisy, out we went." Fried also remembered children running up and down the staircases and sometimes attempting to slide down a banister.[25]

Even though until the 1920s women could not be formal members unless widowed, nor could they vote on congregational issues, they had an influence on the architecture and space of the synagogue as early as 1891. They adhered to the policy of separation of the sexes, entering through their own doors, meeting women friends in their own vestibules, and shepherding their children up the staircases; however, they did not accept the curtains and drew them aside to see the services and observe the activity below.

Wheatley assigned an artist to sketch the congregation at prayer, and the resulting image, the only interior rendering of the Eldridge Street Synagogue from the nineteenth century, lends visual form to his thesis that the immigrants desired both to preserve tradition and to adapt to their surroundings. But the artist, though permitted to observe the Sabbath congregation, was not allowed to sketch on the Sabbath. Rather, he was invited to return on a subsequent weekday. In the final drawing, which was given the better part of a page in the *Century* magazine,

Staircase to the Women's Balcony
   Twin staircases spiral up to the women's balcony. Miriam Aaron, a girl in the 1920s, remembers "a kind of movement to the way the staircase was built." Each staircase was "beautifully shaped," and from being smoothed by many hands, the banister "seemed to glow." (Oral history interview of Miriam Aaron, conducted by Renee Newman, 1995, Collection of the Museum at Eldridge Street.) Photograph © 2007 by Kate Milford.

prayer-shawl-clad congregants engaging enthusiastically in prayer also sport fashionable top hats. Wheatley's accompanying text contains rich, almost anthropological descriptions of the prayer services depicted in the drawing: "Voluminous of voice and ceaseless in gentle movements, articulate worship alternating between the murmurous play of sunlit waves and the thunder of Oriental hurricane, they suggest the idea of an Arab tribe," albeit a tribe boasting "courteous and instructive" congregants, a "superb" choir, and a beautiful house of worship.

The bimah featured in Wheatley's article and partly visible in the drawing is in the center of the sanctuary, a location that reflects adherence to tradition as recorded in the Shulkhan Arukh, the sixteenth-century code of Jewish law and prescriptions. Most Reform synagogues built in America in the 1880s moved the bimah toward the front of the sanctuary in deference to the Protestant practice of placing the reading podium in the front of the congregation and thereby encouraging a certain orderliness and attentiveness. Although the Eldridge Street con-

READING FROM THE SCROLL.

Service in the Sanctuary

    This nineteenth-century drawing depicts congregants during a service. They wear traditional prayer shawls, and some added fashionable top hats. From Richard Wheatley, "The Jews in New York," *Century Magazine*, January 1892.

gregation and the other Orthodox congregations in the neighborhood maintained the tradition of the central bimah, they did modify some of the attendant ritual practices in an attempt to instill a sense of decorum during services: "The [bimah], or pulpit is in the middle of the edifice. There his [the cantor's] assistant conducts the reading of the Torah, or law. Each worshipper may listen to his cantillation thereof, or to the voices of persons successively called out of the congregation, not to read each his part of Torah, Haphtorah, or Megilloth, as in former years, but to see that the *Parasha* is duly recited by the assistant chazan, and to repeat the *B'rachah,* or blessing." What Wheatley describes here is the reading of the Torah, the essential part of the Jewish service. At the Eldridge Street Synagogue, however, the congregation introduced a key innovation: rather than having seven individual members ascend to the bimah to read the parashah, or section of the Torah, as in former years, they now had the cantor or his assistant read it, allowing the other voices to chime in only to recite the blessing on the reading. That is, the congregation eliminated the sound of different voices leading the services, striving instead for uniformity. This subtle change positioned the Eldridge Street bimah at a nexus between tradition and Americanization.

Although the reading of the Torah itself was sacrosanct, the rituals and ceremonies associated with it were open to debate. In general, Jewish congregations in the United States, whether Reform or Orthodox, whether of Sephardic, central, or east European backgrounds, strove over time for order in their respective sanctuaries, an order like that in the contemporary religious spaces of America's Protestant middle class. Jewish congregations thus strengthened the role of a prayer leader (cantor), discouraged stray conversations, and encouraged prayer in unison. While this engagement with decorum was part of a universal process affecting all Jewish congregations to some degree or other, how a particular congregation dealt with the associated tensions offers insight into its character and the issues it faced. Precisely because the Eldridge Street Synagogue maintained so many core elements of the tradition, such as the use of Hebrew, the unabridged prayer book, and the central bimah, what changed and what was debated often represent important responses to American culture. The Eldridge Street Synagogue's congregation strove for respectability but also savored its particular traditions.[26]

Most of the Eldridge Street congregation's negotiations with American decorum involved cosmetic matters, such as the assignment of seats, the donning of top hats, and the strategic stationing of spittoons. Assigned seating meant that people could go directly to their seats, and by mandating that "no conversations shall be held" and appointing trustees to enforce this, with fines if necessary, the congregation hoped that the sanctuary would inspire the right atmosphere for prayer. Curbing conversation was apparently difficult to achieve in practice, as evidenced by the multiple references in the constitution to enforcing "order and decorum" and the provisions for congregants' "disobedience of [trustees'] orders."[27]

Top hats and spittoons, though not mandated by the constitution, had a role in setting a proper tone. Ledgers dating to 1882 show that the congregation prioritized the purchase of spittoons while still on Allen Street and bought annual replacements in August and September in advance of the Jewish New Year. In the late nineteenth century, when snuff taking was considered fashionable, spittoons were commonly found in American homes and public spaces.[28] Adding spittoons to the synagogue sanctuary in no way interfered with Jewish law or custom and in certain respects seemed to encourage the observance of Jewish law. Since Sabbath law forbids the kindling of fire, cigarette-smoking and cigar-smoking immigrants had to rely on snuff to assuage their tobacco craving one day a week. Inhaling snuff appeased those addicted to tobacco, helping them endure the lengthy services, but it also induced a need to spit—hence the spittoons. Mordecai Kaplan, who became one of the most famous rabbis of the twentieth century, a professor at the Jewish Theological Seminary, and the founder of the Reconstructionist movement, attended the Eldridge Street Synagogue with his family in the 1890s, and he remembered the sanctuary as "strong with the smell of snuff." "Every once in a while someone would help himself to [snuff from the box located in a compartment on the bimah] in the course of prayers."[29]

In striving for a decorous and orderly atmosphere, the Eldridge Street congregation tackled the unwieldy controversial practice of *shnodering*. Indeed, auctioning Torah honors seems more appropriate to a Hester Street storefront synagogue than to the Eldridge Street Synagogue's elegant sanctuary, and many of the more established uptown American synagogues had abandoned it because it lengthened the prayer service and had the potential to exacerbate class tensions.[30] In the shnodering system, designated leaders—at Eldridge Street, the president

Spittoons
When taking snuff was popular, ceramic spittoons were
ordered every September before the High Holidays. Photograph
© 2006 by Kate Milford.

and the vice president, or, in later years, the sexton — stood at the bimah and sold *aliyahs*, or Torah honors. The winner of the auction ascended to the bimah to recite the Torah blessing that day, and the cantor or the sexton chanted the appropriate section of the Torah. Recitation and chant were repeated seven times, until the entire parashah had been read. Shnodering provided members with the opportunity to make offerings in honor of those who had blessed the Torah, the *mishebeyrakhs*. The proceeds from the auction usually went to the synagogue, although on special occasions the money was given to particular charities.

Snuffbox

A compartment on the bimah contained snuff for those who wanted tobacco on the Sabbath, when it was forbidden to strike a fire. Photograph © 2006 by Kate Milford.

Shnodering proved to be an effective fundraiser. The practice could bring in more than $150 on Rosh Hashanah; and on less lucrative non-holiday weeks, it could raise $60 or so. Even in August, when, according to the minute books, the wealthy members of the congregation were away on vacations, decreasing the number of members likely to raise bids, shnodering could still bring in a healthy $27.50. Shnodering's potential for raising both funds and the level of indecorum was fully met at a Sabbath Torah service in 1899, when two honorees fought over the order of their blessings, and Israel David Gutman, a trustee, put an end to the fray by lifting the Torah and ending the Torah service. Gutman's effort to restore decorum may have been prompted by a desire to move the service along (or by disgust with the petty fighting), but at a trustees' meeting the following week, he was confronted by President Nathan Hutkoff, who declared that his actions had cost the synagogue "a few dollars in damages." A fight ensued, with Gutman "answer[ing] the president with the greatest rudeness and with the basest of swear words which cannot even be written down on paper." In the end, a committee deemed Gutman's action "a disturbance of the peace" and fined him $18.[31]

As Gutman's case indicates, a decorum-driven congregation could maintain the shnodering system to raise money, but there seem to have been additional, more positive associations with shnodering. Besides opening people's wallets, shnodering also captured people's attention in a profound way. With members publicly negotiating for ceremonial roles, shnodering shifted the congregants' eyes from their prayer books to the bimah to watch brothers, fathers, husbands, and neighbors taking part in the auction. Viewers could gauge who was doing well, who was doing less well, who was generous or not, and could observe a family celebrating a joyous occasion or a special guest, such as Chief Rabbi Jacob Joseph.[32] Family pride and loyalty could be affirmed by bidding for honors. Rose Eisenberg recalled her father's successful bid for the entire set of aliyahs, to be distributed among the family. Although the well-to-do members participated on a more regular basis and donated more to the pledging than did less well-off members, at least five people bid an affordable fifty cents or a dollar each week. Indeed, until 1915 every member participated at least once or twice a year, for membership entailed a minimum yearly contribution through aliyahs. In the last decade of the nineteenth century and the first decade of the twentieth, the constitution stipulated a four-dollar contribution; the new constitution in 1913 decreased the amount to two dollars. Even for those who did not pledge, being there to observe the auction was a key to keeping up with congregational politics. And every worshipper had a stake in the success of the auctions, for the proceeds benefited the synagogue.

The decrease in the amount of required contributions to aliyahs in 1913 signaled a shift in the fundraising potential of shnodering. Although the practice still brought in money on a weekly basis, the requirement that members contribute a certain amount hampered membership drives. Early in 1915 a member speculated that the required annual pledge of $2 might be deterring potential members from joining: "Small societies or individual people might perhaps wish to belong to the synagogue but they are afraid of the high cost of pledges in a large synagogue." A month or so later, a committee proposed restricting Sabbath pledges to the Maftir section of the Torah reading, which would allow only one aliyah to be auctioned off every week, but this change was deemed too radical. Finally the congregation agreed to ban mishebeyrakhs except on holidays, but they retained the core of the shnodering system, the sale of Sabbath, High Holiday, and festival aliyahs. To meet the challenge of recruiting members, they waived the requirement that new members participate in the system and publicized the shift: "Resolved to advertise in the paper and also to hang up a sign that the synagogue is taking new members without charging an entrance or pledge fee. Only an annual fee of 10.00 will be charged."[33] So integral had the shnodering system become to congregational ritual that its dismissal could not be countenanced, even in the face of opposition and potentially negative financial consequences. Their willingness to modify it, rather than dismiss it altogether, shows that their attachment to the system was not solely an economic one.

The shnodering system prevailed on the Lower East Side for many years despite its potential for encouraging indecorum, and congregations like Eldridge Street took advantage of innovations to preserve the system and reap its financial benefits. One of the problems posed by the shnodering system in a large congregation was how to record the names, pledges, and addresses of bidding nonmembers without violating the Sabbath laws, which prohibited writing as well as the exchange of money. One solution was to use S. H. Isaacs' Ring Tape Recording Chart, which allowed the necessary information to be entered for each aliyah in turn without writing. A set of columns represented the person's name, another set the address, another set the amount, and so forth. Each of the seven columns under "Name of Person," for example, contained the alphabet, letter by letter. By moving adjustable elastic rings up or down, column by column, to the proper letters, the secretary could "spell" out the name. After the Sabbath the secretary could transfer the data into a ledger, organized by week and by the name of the Torah section, and could collect the money pledged. Once he finished recording, he could pull the elastic rings back to the top, clearing the chart for the next Sabbath. Isaacs's invention reflected the desire to give the shnodering system a certain staying power in America, and the ingenuity applied to modifying the system went a long way toward keeping the ritual.[34]

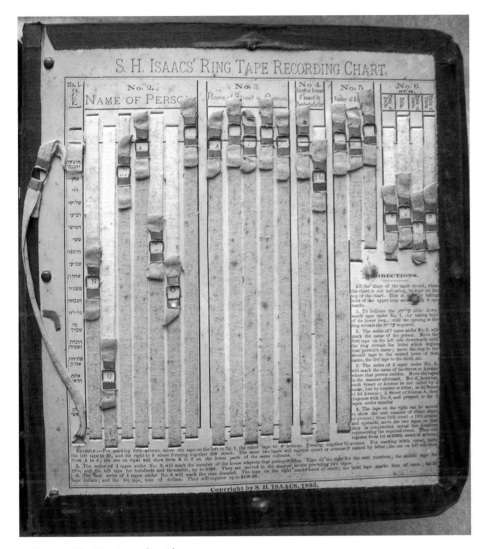

S. H. Isaacs' Ring Tape Recording Chart

This unique ledger, patented by S. H. Isaacs, enabled Orthodox congregations to record the pledges made at the Torah service without violating Sabbath laws on writing. The secretary could slide the rings to spell out the pledge information. Courtesy of the American Jewish Historical Society.

Pledge Ledger

After the Sabbath, the secretary transferred pledge information from the ring tape recording chart into a simple ledger, and the rings were brought back to the top, ready for the next Sabbath.

Seated on the balcony in an early decade of the twentieth century, Gussie Dubrin could watch her father, Morris Dubrin, the longtime sexton, call out the names of those who would make an aliyah. The congregation held a "very quiet, very orderly" service. Members settled in their assigned seats, trustees maintained peace, and officers on the bimah dispensed Torah honors in an organized fashion, with the secretary recording the details. Richard Wheatley noted the "indulgence in talk" but emphasized the dignity of the congregation. The rare mention in the minutes of specific outbursts suggests that most of the time worshippers obeyed the synagogue's constitution. Even when disruptions occurred, they tended to happen during meetings or outside the synagogue and not during the prayer services themselves.[35]

There had been many changes since the noisy gathering at the dedication of the synagogue. Between 1887 and 1915 the congregation transformed the space of the sanctuary by removing the curtains of the women's balcony, diversified its membership, democratized its leadership, and modified the shnodering system, all in response to life in America and, specifically, the changing demographic of the Lower East Side. Longtime leaders like Sender Jarmulowsky, David Cohen, and Nathan Hutkoff moved uptown, leaving others to adopt new methods of running the congregation and recruiting members. Still, the early leaders' commitment and devotion to the congregation set a powerful precedent, one that later leaders emulated.

SIX

Patriarchs and Matriarchs

N *GHETTO SILHOUETTES*, a 1902 book about the Lower East Side, David War-field describes the neighborhood's "revered institution" as a bank, not a syna-gogue, and its "patriarch" as a banker, not a rabbi. At the bank, the faithful masses come "to deposit or withdraw, to borrow or indorse," rather than to study or to pray. "Jobblelousky's bank," he writes, "is a revered institution of the East Side. It started in prehistoric times, that is to say, before the beginning of the great Russian immigration. The head of the house was a patriarchal gentleman, who owned sev-eral blocks of houses, all free and clear of encumbrance. His sons and sons-in-law, all neatly dressed, polite and energetic, were clerks, book-keepers and cashiers in the establishment. Incidentally, everyone of them was also the owner of real estate." Jobblelousky was very rich. "Certainly, he was worth a million dollars, and his income rolled in very much as the waters of the Hudson sweep into the sea. He was the banker of the East Side. There are banks and bankers over there, and while they did business in the hundreds, Jobblelousky did it in the thousands. The Chemical Bank, which is the most conservative in the world, put his note on a par with Uncle Sam."[1]

In a sense, this sketch underlines a shift in values in the immigrant commu-nity. In eastern Europe the Jewish masculine ideal had been a scholar well versed in Hebrew texts, primed to receive and interpret the teachings of past generations and pass them on to the future generations, but in America what counted was the ability to bestow dollars and real estate upon the next generation. Warfield modeled the character of Jobblelousky on the real-life Sender Jarmulowsky, the Lower East Side's successful banker and the Eldridge Street Synagogue's first president. Although Warfield focused on Jarmulowsky's American business success, the Yiddish press emphasized other aspects of his character and biography: that he was a Sabbath-observant scholar, a graduate of the famed Lithuanian Talmudic academy (yeshiva) of Volozhin, and one of the greatest educational philanthropists of the East Side. As the *Morgn zhurnal* put it, "Jarmulowsky was living proof that in America one can be a rich businessman but also be a true, pious Jew."[2] Indeed, these two aspects of his identity — business and piety — were fused in his role as president of the Eldridge Street Synagogue.

On the Lower East Side, the role of business in synagogue life was both necessary and controversial — necessary because the formation of congregations and the purchase of synagogue property demanded financial contributions, and controversial because often those contributions enabled men with little Jewish education to become the synagogue's lay leaders. Critics excoriated such lay leaders. According to one, the wealthy in America were the "worst element," the "coarse ones who know from the Torah and from Judaism as much as a hen knows from being a person."[3] Still, the Yiddish press eventually came to understand and even appreciate the relationship between Jobblelousky's business acumen and Jarmulowsky's piety and philanthropy, fashioning in consequence a complex and nuanced portrait of an emerging American Jewish masculine ideal. This idealized figure, at once scholarly, energetic, and business-oriented, was a model for Eldridge Street's pioneer presidents and had a profound impact on the Jewish community as a whole.

When in prayer at Eldridge Street, most presidents took seats of honor along the eastern wall. This privilege undoubtedly caused resentment among members of the congregation who could not afford the ticket price of such seats or who thought that these seats of honor should be linked to scholarship, not money. But the presidents who sat there sought more than purchased glory and were being recognized for far more than the checks they wrote to support the synagogue. Jarmulowsky, Isaac Gellis, David Cohen, and Nathan Hutkoff conducted the business of the congregation in the bes medresh, which doubled as a meeting room. There, gavel in hand, they raised money, negotiated mergers, arbitrated disputes, exam-

Bench along the Eastern Wall
    Wooden benches built into the eastern wall of the sanctuary on either side of the ark were seats of honor. Each seat had a stand for prayer books. The congregation reserved several seats for rabbis or prominent visitors, but lay leaders purchased the majority of the eastern wall seats. Photograph by Edward Cheng.

ined construction contracts, and maintained the synagogue in other ways. They also sponsored visiting rabbis, hired scholars to teach adult classes, raised money for yeshivas, made gifts of Hebrew books, collected endowments for widows, and debated the qualifications of prospective cantors. When congregation collections did not suffice, they reached into their own pockets to offer gifts and no-interest loans.[4] They hired Rabbi Yosef Eliyahu Fried to teach classes in the bes medresh and honored him, too, with a seat along the eastern wall. The presidents' painstaking and innovative management of congregational affairs, like the physical pillars visible in the lower bes medresh, provided support for the majestic sanctuary above and created a home for the religious life of hundreds of congregants.

    The contributions and legacies of the Eldridge Street Synagogue's first four presidents — Jarmulowsky, Gellis, Cohen, and Hutkoff — highlight the importance of business and religion in the development of both the synagogue and the Lower East Side community. During their terms as president, these men also helped to

Bes Medresh

The bes medresh was a home for daily prayer and study; it was also where the biweekly trustees' meetings and monthly members' meetings were convened. During the meetings the lay leaders discussed finances, building repairs, and communal issues. Photograph © 2007 by Kate Milford.

establish and shape some of the principal communal institutions in New York that addressed both the immediate and the long-term needs of the immigrant community, including shelters to assist newly arrived immigrants, neighborhood hospitals, Hebrew schools, congregational associations, and communal government structures.[5] Neither narrow-minded scholars nor uneducated merchants, men like these drew inspiration from the transplanted east European ideals of scholarship and piety but applied their business acumen to the establishment and direction of the institutions necessary for bringing east European Orthodoxy to America.

As yeshiva scholar, banker, and synagogue president, Sender Jarmulowsky encapsulated the multitude of traits and skills that enabled the early leaders to successfully plant traditional Jewish values in American soil. Born in 1841 in Drajewo, in the Lomza province of Russia (now part of Poland), Jarmulowsky was orphaned at the age of three and raised by the Rabbi of Werblow. Impressed with his intellect, the rabbi sent him to the famed Volozhin Yeshiva, an elite Talmudic academy. Jarmulowsky emerged from the yeshiva with rabbinical ordination and impressive scholarly credentials and, though penniless, was selected to be the groom of Rebecca Markels, the daughter of a wealthy merchant. The linkage of scholarship with wealth constituted the classic match in east European Jewish society and enabled the scholar to pursue his studies on a full-time basis. Yet Jarmulowsky opted to enter the business world instead. As the *Morgn zhurnal* reported, "He could have taken a rabbinical position but did not want to earn a living from the Torah." In 1868 Jarmulowsky moved to Hamburg where he established a successful passage and exchange business to transfer goods and people across the Atlantic Ocean. In 1873, at the age of thirty-two, he opened a second office in New York.

Jarmulowsky's business flourished in New York, and by the turn of the century he was rumored to be a millionaire. Well known in both Europe and the United States, Jarmulowsky had status and connections that perhaps assisted in the migration process. "Sender Jarmulowsky was a name that was known to every Jew in the old and also in the new world," wrote the *Tageblat*. "His business brought him into contact with hundreds of thousands of immigrants to whom the name Jarmulowsky was the guarantee of honesty." Once in America, immigrants could make use of his bank as they saved money to send for relatives, purchase steamship tickets for their relatives, or open their own businesses. In turn, Jarmulowsky funneled his own funds and expertise back into the community. While the Orthodox Yiddish press celebrated the traditional knowledge that Jarmulowsky brought with him—his Talmudic knowledge was proclaimed a "treasure"—Jarmulowsky seemed to understand the importance of reconceiving Jewish education for the American setting; he disbursed funds to various educational organizations, funded private individuals, and sought to create an overarching community board.[6] Early on, he spearheaded the efforts of the Association of Orthodox Hebrew Congregations, the organization that later brought over Chief Rabbi Jacob Joseph. Following the disbandment of the association, Jarmulowsky supported the Orthodox Union and the Jewish Theological Seminary and served on the executive board of the Kehillah (Jewish Community of New York). So integral was Jarmulowsky's "work for unity among Jews," that upon his death the Kehillah's executive board held an emergency meeting "to discuss this great loss to the Jews of New York."[7]

Entrance Arch on S. Jarmulowsky's Bank
    When completed in 1912, Sender Jarmulowsky's twelve-story bank was among the tallest buildings on the Lower East Side, and its interior rivaled those of uptown banks. The date carved into the archway, 1873, acknowledges the bank's long history at the corner of Canal and Orchard Streets. Photograph by Rachel Rabhan.

According to accounts in the Orthodox Yiddish press, Jarmulowsky's legacy was much larger than the money he gave or the expertise he offered. He set an example in a young community where men of action were needed, not just to succeed in America but to build the institutions—synagogues, educational centers, and governing bodies—necessary for adapting east European Orthodoxy to the American setting. As the Yiddish press often pointed out, pioneers like Jarmulowsky assisted with "advice and with action." To build new Jewish institutions required neither a full-time scholar nor a full-time businessman but a man experienced in both worlds: Jarmulowsky "was an East Side businessman of the best kind, a Jew from whom the younger generation of businessmen can learn the duties and obligations that such a position has for Russian Jewish immigrants in America."[8]

Jarmulowsky's defining contribution to the Eldridge Street Synagogue was the energy with which he rallied his fellow congregants to build the first great house of worship for east European Jews in the United States. Only a man of Jarmulowsky's financial stature and business acumen could have orchestrated such an expensive and risky move. During a remarkable three-year period, he harnessed the fortunes of Kahal Adath Jeshurun to build its magnificent synagogue and enlisted the enthusiasm and expertise of Isaac Gellis, David Cohen, and Nathan Hutkoff, who each succeeded him as president. Jarmulowsky's ambitions linked the congregation to communal efforts beyond this real-estate venture. Sabbaths were set aside to raise money for the Volozhin Yeshiva, back in Russia, and the synagogue was used as a meeting hall to gather subscriptions for the Agudes Hakehillos. For the goal of bringing over a chief rabbi, the congregation pledged an annual payment of $350, the second-highest pledge made by any of the participating congregations.[9] Under the leadership of Jarmulowsky and his successors, the Eldridge Street congregation fundraised for Yeshiva Etz Chaim and other local Hebrew schools and, when necessary, offered them classroom space at the synagogue.

Although Jarmulowsky moved uptown in 1889, his prominence and community involvement set a precedent that future presidents followed. They, too, often took on leadership roles in large-scale community efforts, such as the Hebrew Sheltering Society, the Orthodox Union, the Kehillah, and local yeshivas. They, too, often used the Eldridge Street Synagogue as a communal meeting hall to serve the needs of these organizations and, in doing so, kept the congregation's profile as visible and distinctive as its prominent synagogue structure.

If Jarmulowsky's passage and exchange office helped to bring immigrants to New York, Isaac Gellis's business helped provide them with a key necessity for Orthodox Jewish life once here: kosher meat. Gellis arrived in New York in 1870 at the age of twenty. The Yiddish press later described the New York of the time as a veritable "wilderness," with very few institutions to cater to Orthodox Jews. Gellis forged a Jewish trail through this wilderness, emerging as the "pioneer in the manufacture of kosher provisions." An advertisement celebrating the sixtieth anniversary of the Gellis Sausage Company showed how his business had proved integral in allowing Judaism to flourish in America: The sausage company "is older than the oldest Yiddish newspapers; older than almost all of the Orthodox

Main Office of Isaac Gellis and Company
After Isaac Gellis's death in 1906, his thirty-three-year-old sausage business
passed into the hands of his wife, Sarah, and sons, Harry, Samuel, and Charles.
Courtesy of the American Jewish Historical Society.

synagogues; older than ALL of the existing Jewish institutions; older by ten years
than the Jewish mass immigration from Russia and Poland." As proprietor of "one
of the oldest Jewish businesses in New York," it was Isaac Gellis, rather than a rabbi
or an editor, who eased the immigrant transition to America in the 1880s by providing "good, real, kosher meat products."[10] Although this advertisement, printed
almost thirty years after his death, might have overstated his influence, attendance
at his funeral in 1906 testified to his communal importance. When Gellis died,

more than thirteen thousand mourners gathered at the Eldridge Street Synagogue to pay their respects. Three thousand of them squeezed into the synagogue to hear the eulogies of five rabbis while the remaining throng "stood outside with bared heads" to mourn the man who had been a member of "every Hebrew charitable institution."[11] Although Jarmulowsky and, later, Cohen and Hutkoff all moved uptown and formed or joined congregations in their new neighborhoods, Gellis remained on the Lower East Side and was the sole pioneering president to have his funeral at the synagogue.

Gellis was as much a pioneer during his tenure as synagogue president at Eldridge Street as he was in his own business. Serving as vice president in 1894 and holding the presidency for two terms, from 1895 to 1897, Gellis inherited Jarmulowsky's vision but also the financial responsibility of synagogue leadership, including enormous costs that he often assumed himself. A few months after Gellis became the vice president, the congregation discussed a loan coming due from Jarmulowsky's time, and the minutes record the resolution: "Mr. Yitskhok Gellis stands up and undertakes to pay." A month later, Gellis offered another $1,000 in loans to the congregation, and in April 1895, when President David Cohen called a special meeting to discuss notes in the value of $4,000 that were due the next day, saying that "the brothers should do something about it," Cohen, Gellis, and Hutkoff cosigned the loans.[12]

Although the presidents' financial support was crucial during the early years, the executive position also demanded a familiarity with real estate and Jewish and American law, plus a gift for balancing routine and unanticipated demands. During Gellis's two-year presidency, he oversaw the painting of the synagogue, auditioned cantors, fixed the rooftop finials, settled disputes among members, delivered eulogies, visited the sick, and presided over all general, special, and trustee meetings. When it was brought to Gellis's attention that dozens of holy books were in severe disrepair, "he declared that we must remove the damaged fragments of holy scriptures from the cellar" and organized an outing to the Bayside Cemetery in Queens so that the books could be buried according to Jewish law. Gellis arranged for Rabbi Yosef Fried to officiate, required all officers and trustees to attend, and invited "all who wished to take part in the Mitzva." The journey to the Queens cemetery in February's cold, carrying dusty books, took the better part of a Sunday.[13] For many synagogue presidents and officers, serving the synagogue was not just an extension of business but the expression of a desire to live a pious life.

When pressures spurred David Cohen or, later, Nathan Hutkoff each to threaten resignation on three separate occasions, the congregation pleaded with them to stay. When urged to run for a third term, Gellis declined, explaining that he could "no longer carry the burden of office because of the burden of his own business matters." Nevertheless, like the next two presidents, Cohen and Hutkoff, Gellis remained intimately involved with the management of the congregation following his official retirement from office. At various points, Gellis and his fellow ex-presidents expressed concern over the state of the building, understanding that the upkeep of the synagogue was essential to attract new members. To this end, Gellis supervised the hiring, contracting, and accounting needed to repair the synagogue windows and the roof; he also served on a committee of ten that "had full authority to do everything for the welfare of our congregation."[14]

Hiring laborers, contracting with cantors, and presiding over meetings consumed the energy of the pioneer presidents, but their commitment to details and their forethought ensured that the congregation functioned properly and the synagogue maintained its beauty. Their work had tangible results, for it kept the synagogue open for daily prayer. From their seats of honor, the pioneers could observe the congregation at prayer and enjoy the beauty of the synagogue they worked for.[15] In turn, the congregation appreciated the continued presence at services of Isaac Gellis, one of the last pioneers to remain in the neighborhood after the turn of the century. His personal and financial investments in the synagogue ensured his patriarchal presence along the eastern wall.

For the first twenty-five years of Kahal Adath Jeshurun's existence, the name David A. Cohen was ever present in the synagogue minutes. Cohen maintained an active involvement in the congregation during and after his three presidential terms, chairing committees, reminding members of constitutional rules, and offering gifts and loans. He spent time in the bes medresh engaged in study; although he arrived in America at the age of fourteen, his studies in New York gained him status as a *bar urin*, or scholar. Cohen's special gift to the Jewish community, however, was his knowledge of real estate, which he used to assist the development of the Eldridge Street Synagogue and Jewish educational institutions, first on the Lower East Side and later in Harlem and other new Jewish neighborhoods. Cohen may have been responsible for securing the first two lots on Eldridge Street—numbers 14 and 16—which his Congregation Holkhe Yosher Vizaner brought to the table upon the 1886 merger with Beth Hamedrash. It is also possible that Cohen selected the synagogue's architects, for his real-estate firm was located a few doors down from the Herter Brothers on Broadway. Certainly, Cohen played an integral role in the building of the synagogue and was singled out for special mention by President Sender Jarmulowsky upon its completion.[16]

Cohen, thirty-three in 1887, seems to have learned from Jarmulowsky's example, for he devoted his attention to the Eldridge Street Synagogue but also contributed to a variety of outside charities, especially those with educational missions, including the Uptown Talmud Torah, the Bronx Machzike Talmud Torah, and the Hebrew Teachers Institute. The Orthodox Yiddish press hailed Cohen as a "diligent community doer" who used his business success in America to not only support but help establish new organizations. The *Morgn zhurnal* claimed that "such active Jewish workers build the bridge that binds the past generation of immigrants to the present, and they make it so one can continue the work in the future."[17]

Cohen, who arrived from Suwalk in 1868, played an important role in the development of the Jewish institutions on the Lower East Side, but by the 1890s, he could see how neighborhoods in Brooklyn, the Upper East Side, and especially Harlem were emerging as new residential areas for immigrant Jews and their children. Movement away from the Lower East Side was inevitable; as transportation became available and new areas beckoned, thousands of overcrowded Lower East Side residents seized the opportunity to live in a more commodious neighborhood. Seventy-five percent of New York's Jews lived on the Lower East Side in 1892, but only 50 percent did by 1903, and only 23 percent by 1916. This movement had a marked effect on congregational membership; although incoming immigration kept the Lower East Side Jewish population steady, the exodus to Harlem, Brooklyn, and the Bronx swept up many members of the wealthier class, often those who had provided congregational leadership. Many of them, such as Jarmulowsky, who helped organize Zichron Ephraim on East Sixty-seventh Street in 1889, devoted their energies to establishing new synagogues near their residences. In 1907 a Yiddish newspaper acknowledged as "an 'open secret'" the fact that Lower East Side congregations suffered "as the wealthier householders moved to other parts of the city."[18]

A real-estate man with deep personal ties to the Eldridge Street Synagogue, Cohen must have been torn when he, too, decided to move to Harlem. Although he kept his offices downtown and could still pray on Eldridge Street during the week and attend all meetings, he needed to find a new congregation for Sabbath and holiday prayer, for Jewish law prohibits travel on those days. Observing the movement uptown of fellow Eldridge Street Synagogue members and institutions, Cohen probably came up with the idea of building an uptown branch of the synagogue, in a typical blend of business sense and devotion to Jewish institutional life. Because the movement of the well-to-do people out of the Lower East Side portended opportunity elsewhere, the time was ripe for a branch synagogue to both shore up support for the home synagogue and successfully found an offshoot of the established congregation. The minutes of May 1903 report a "debate concerning the establishment of an uptown branch of the synagogue. Since there were no actual plans, nothing was decided."[19]

The minutes do not specify whether it was Cohen who proposed the idea, but they do suggest the congregation's interest in the prospect and imply an acknowledgment of the need to address the movement of residents away from the neighborhood. By 1907, the next time the issue was officially raised, a congregation made up of Eldridge Street Synagogue members had started to gather for prayer uptown and had produced "actual plans" to buy a building. Cohen, who by now lived at 49 West 113th Street, was one of several who proposed an extension of the name, along with funding, to the Harlem congregation. At the suggestion of members who had moved uptown, committees were formed at the Eldridge Street Synagogue to investigate the founding of an uptown branch. In November 1908, "a large majority was present and the matter of a branch was declared to be a benefit for our congregation."[20]

Even as the congregation considered formally supporting an uptown branch, it sought to bolster its downtown membership, and in October 1908, Nathan Hutkoff, who, like Cohen, had also moved uptown but also remained active downtown, proposed advertising "that we wish to have societies join us, with very easy conditions." A committee was formed to explore mergers with other downtown congregations, and a few months later, in January 1909, Hutkoff advised a merger with Anshe Lubz (People of Lubz). The union reinvigorated the congregation, adding 125 new members, $3,500, and two cemetery lots to the Eldridge Street Synagogue's holdings. Those involved in the uptown branch movement must have approved the merger, for several of them, including David Cohen, joined the committee responsible for making arrangements for the merger, which met at Cohen's home a month later to plan the merger ceremonies.[21] Strengthening the congregation as a whole and enhancing its financial capacity would, it was thought, assist efforts to found an uptown branch.

The men of the Lubz congregation, now part of the Eldridge Street congregation, thought otherwise and in July 1909 held a special meeting to vote for or against support of the uptown branch. "A debate was held concerning this. It was resolved to hold a vote by ballot to decide whether or not to establish a branch. With this, the special meeting was closed with the resolution that no branch should be established."[22] Although the vote meant that the Eldridge Street Synagogue could not acknowledge a formal connection with the uptown branch that was eventually established, it nonetheless lent the uptown congregation five Torah scrolls and its members were officially invited to the synagogue dedication.

The Eldridge Street members who wanted an uptown branch took action. On October 30, David Cohen filed a temporary injunction contesting the legality of the merger with Anshe Lubz and barring the Eldridge Street Synagogue from conducting business. Later the Eldridge Street congregation wrote that "they tried to make peace" with the members of the Cohen-led faction "by all possible means. They brought rabbis and also people to negotiate, several times, but they were unsuccessful in settling peacefully. They were finally obliged to take a lawyer and to go to the gentile court of law."[23] The conflict spiraled into the realm of rabbinical arbitration and then to the New York State Supreme Court.

In April 1911, Judge Edward McCall ruled against Cohen's contingent, finding that not only was the merger legal but Cohen himself had approved it. The judge further argued that the contingent favoring a branch synagogue on 113th Street had only contested the merger when they learned that the consolidated congregation would not fund the new synagogue. The judge said: "We can lay our finger right upon the actual cause of all of this trouble, and that is, the making of a proposition by Mr. Cohen that the consolidated congregation loan its money and permit the use of its name to aid the 113th Street synagogue, and the refusal on the part of the consolidated congregation to consent to either proposition."[24]

On April 14 the *Forverts* splashed McCall's decision on its front page: "The long controversy between the downtown congregation and the 'allrightniks' of uptown ended with a victory for the downtowners."[25] A socialist paper did not usually address synagogue politics; however, the editors viewed this as less a religious matter than a matter of class tensions. In this case, the paper could celebrate a neighborhood institution that had successfully fended off the intrusions of uptown allrightniks. Given the rapid loss of residents who moved uptown, the common experience of living on the Lower East Side often transcended ideological differences between the pious and the freethinkers.

At Eldridge Street, the triumph of the court case was bittersweet; after all, this challenge had come from within, from members who had called each other "brothers" for decades, and tension was heightened by David Cohen's death the week after the verdict was rendered. Cohen's funeral was held uptown at the Harlem Synagogue, but the funeral procession stopped at the Eldridge Street Synagogue, which the Yiddish press credited Cohen with founding. That week, the downtown congregation convened, and "the vice-president, Avrohom Fein, opened the meeting in the name of Kahal Adath Jeshurun and Anshe Lubz and asked all the brothers to stand up in order to pay their respects to the deceased brother David Cohen." The congregation unanimously accepted Nathan Hutkoff's proposal "that peace should be made and that there should be no more quarreling or divisions. A committee should be appointed to resolve all claims peacefully and once again peace should reign . . . for the good and welfare of the congregation."[26] This subdued reaction to the resolution of the eighteen-month conflict was surely due to Cohen's recent death, which prompted consideration of his motivations and his attachment to the Eldridge Street Synagogue. Despite moving uptown, Cohen and others had invested heavily in the congregation, both emotionally and financially, and yearned for the sustained brotherhood a formal alliance would convey.

Although in many ways the court case signaled a rejection of the authority and control, once so crucial, of individual leaders like Cohen, it also affirmed confidence in the downtown synagogue and its leadership, and this was due in part to the continued advice and mentorship of Nathan Hutkoff. It was Hutkoff, in his capacity as treasurer, who had advised the merger with Anshe Lubz. The result of the merger, affirmed by the court case, was that the two congregations would share leadership, expanding the number of trustees from twelve to eighteen to accommodate the changes, but that Kahal Adath Jeshurun would remain a viable downtown congregation. It found a place of honor and recognition for Anshe Lubz's president, Shimon Lazerowitz, who became president of the merged congregation in the 1912 election. In 1913 the merged congregation printed a new constitution, inscribed with a new name—Kahal Adath Jeshurun and Anshe Lubz—which removed holding a seat as a prerequisite for holding office, lowered the price of seats by a percentage point and decreased the price of membership fees from $14 to $10 a year. Hutkoff, the man who engineered the merger, understood that change was in order.

When the synagogue opened in 1887, Jarmulowsky was forty-seven, Gellis was thirty-seven, Cohen was thirty-three, and Hutkoff was fifty-two. All were relatively young. Thirty years later, when the congregation named Nathan Hutkoff honorary president, he had outlived all the cofounders of the synagogue. Upon his death, the *Morgn zhurnal* outlined Hutkoff's life, pointing out that when he arrived in this country, in 1863, he had encountered only a "small Jewish population, with no sign of the Jewish institutions for which New York is now famous." He promptly set himself up in the plate glass business, then "devoted himself to creating some order in Jewish institutional life."[27] Hutkoff was among the founders of the Hebrew Sheltering Society in 1889, which provided assistance to newly arrived immigrants and also helped prepare immigrants still in eastern Europe for the journey to America. When ninety-six representatives from the United States and Canada convened to form the Orthodox Union at the Eldridge Street Synagogue in 1898, Hutkoff was one of three leaders elected to the union's board of trustees. He also took the reins of the Beth Israel Hospital, which was suffering from the effects of the 1893 depression. According to the *New York Times*, "Mr. Hutkoff accepted the Presidency in June and went to work with a will, greatly improving its financial condition."[28] When he was president of the synagogue, he likewise gave sound financial advice, and he insisted on community involvement.

When Hutkoff moved uptown in 1898, he felt it only fair to resign his position. However, the congregation "unanimously" rejected his resignation and asked their president to "remain in office as long as possible." Hutkoff not only obliged but served an additional term. In appreciation, the congregation gave him a "golden medal with a photograph of the synagogue engraved on it." Hutkoff accepted this gift with gratitude and promised "always to work for the good of the congregation and to remain forever loyal."[29] Hutkoff was true to his words. He headed many committees and undertook the management of the congregation's finances as treasurer. By 1914 the congregation had created the new role of "Honorary President" for Hutkoff.

By the time of Hutkoff's death, in 1917, the immigrant Jews had established hospitals, schools, rabbinical unions, social service agencies, and synagogues, all of which helped them lead observant lives in America. Though significant, the institutions promoted by the pioneer presidents were not their greatest legacy. In their obituaries, the Orthodox Yiddish press spoke of the early days of immigration to emphasize the qualities of the men, not only as links in the chain of tradition but also as exceptional activists. The *Tageblat* wrote, "It is entirely natural in wandering from one country to another and finding new circumstances that many of the newcomers abandon all that they were in the old world. It was thus necessary that among the earlier Russian immigrants there were men who held true to Judaism and who showed with their actions that in America one can be a Jew."[30] Jarmulowsky, Hutkoff, Cohen, and Gellis not only held true to Judaism but used their business ability to show with their actions the need to adapt Judaism to America. Decades after their arrival and in the days after their deaths, the immigrant Jewish community still demanded this combination: loyalty to tradition and awareness of secular realities.

Jewish women's contributions were not so memorialized, not for a long time. True, the four great wooden doors of the synagogue, carved with stars of David, are said to represent Judaism's four Matriarchs: Sarah, Rebecca, Rachel, and Leah. But during much of the Eldridge Street Synagogue's early history, the women lacked official recognition. Their status as leaders gradually became formalized

Four Doors

  The four doors of the synagogue are said to symbolize Judaism's four Matriarchs, Sarah, Rebecca, Rachel, and Leah. Men entered through the center doors, women through the northern or southern doors, which led directly to staircases leading to the women's balcony. Photograph by Edward Cheng.

through membership opportunities and, in 1919, the formation of a Ladies' Auxiliary. In 1925 the congregation's own Sarahs, Rebeccas, Rachels, and Leahs, by then named Freyde, Breine, and Hinde, were commemorated architecturally with the installation of a sanctuary-level marble plaque honoring the Ladies' Auxiliary. In general, as business needs eclipsed men's devotions and religious activity, women's home-based religious activity rose in importance. Consequently, as new American Jewish leadership roles emerged that favored public action over scholarship or prayer, women, who had been excluded from major leadership roles in the Jewish community owing to their lack of scholarly training, were able to extend their home-based family and charitable religious practice to social efforts in the congregation and community, actively adapting tradition to the American context as they did so. As the historian Paula Hyman explains, "The values of east European Jewish culture, transplanted to America and gradually transformed by America, permitted women to play a complex role."[31]

One of the first matriarchs of the Eldridge Street Synagogue for whom we have a record is Sarah Gellis, wife of the third president of the synagogue. Sarah was poised to take over the family business after Isaac's death, having helped administer it from the very start. Like her husband, she extended her activities to community endeavors. According to their grandson's recollection, Isaac and Sarah had met on the boat to America. Once in New York, the two married and opened a kosher butcher shop, which they expanded into a kosher sausage firm two years later. "When they first opened the butcher shop she could lug a 400-pound piece of meat and throw it on the slab," recalled her grandson, Abraham Gellis. When the business closed at noon on Fridays, Sarah, who was "very religious," prepared the Sabbath meal for her seven children and other members of the Jewish community, hosted in a two-day open house. With the help of two cooks, she prepared gefilte fish and chicken for both the Friday night and the Saturday day meals. Her grandson recalled the "continuous run of people coming to sit and eat." During Passover, Isaac donated one thousand pounds of kosher meat to the synagogue for their part in the traditional *moes-khitim* communal outreach. Sarah undertook her own charitable endeavors. According to her grandson, "When Passover came along she provided 350 kids with clothes from my grandfather's factory. She went to [a leader] in the shoe business and got 350 pairs of shoes. They all lined up and were measured for the right size. Then she got Phillips, the shirt people, shirts for nothing. She got hat people. She got everyone in the world and they would run this for years. This was her own charitable setup."[32] As an active leader of the Eldridge Street congregation, Isaac could make a significant contribution to a long-established Passover charity through formal channels. Having no such apparatus at her disposal, Sarah created her own.

By virtue of her business connections, Sarah Gellis was able to engage the immigrant community on a large scale, but her activities paralleled those of other immigrant women who made their impact on religious and communal life through Sabbath and holiday preparations and informal charitable deeds. Traditionally, women's religious obligations consist of keeping kosher, preparing for the Sabbath, and visiting the mikvah for ritual cleansing. Since women were not officially members of the Eldridge Street or other synagogues, it is hard to measure their formal religious observance.

Yet memoirs and oral histories of the Lower East Side abound with details of how preparation for and participation in the Friday night Sabbath played a major role in transmitting a Jewish sense of identity for many immigrants. When asked how her family celebrated the Sabbath, Gussie Dubrin did not mention the services her father led in the synagogue. Instead, she emphasized her mother's activities in the home: "My mother lit the candles. On Shabes [Sabbath]—if we didn't have anything for the rest of the week—we had a big meal Friday night." A University Settlement House social worker who surveyed immigrant working families on the East Side found the same to be true for others: "Great preparations are generally made for the Sabbath menu, which is in most cases the only day when meals are taken in degree of regularity." In 1902 a reporter from *The Outlook* wrote, "In the Ghetto, Friday, the day before the Sabbath, is a day of agitation, of scrubbing, cooking, baking."[33]

The cumulative effect of women's preparations for the Friday night Sabbath physically transformed the Lower East Side, improving the appearance of the tenements both inside and out. Richard Wheatley, depicting the woeful conditions in the tenements, conceded that Sabbath preparations improved the "interior rooms that would be more filthy than they are but for the Sabbath." And a *New York Times* reporter wrote, "On Friday afternoon the facades of many of the tenements were almost obscured by pillows and blankets being freshened, in conjunction with other pre-Sabbath sprucing measures."[34]

Women's preparations also increased activity in the streets' pushcart markets. On Thursday nights and Friday mornings, the women of the neighborhood poured into the streets for the weekly rounds of shopping and bargaining. Indeed, so characteristic were the Sabbath preparations that a *New York Times* reporter advised readers curious about the Jews of New York to "step off a Third Avenue car at the corner of Hester Street and the Bowery some Friday morning and walk east along the former street. I say 'Friday morning' because the market, striking and characteristic of the ghetto and its life, is held on that day. This is done so that an ample store of eatables may be laid in for *Shabbes* (The Jewish Sabbath) on the morrow." A reporter for the *New York Daily Tribune* who visited the market on Friday found people "massed so thickly on the pavements that it is only in aggressive fashion that one can make his way through the crowd. As for the middle of the street, there is no middle to be seen."[35]

Immigrant women's religious activities may have caused changes in the neighborhood as well as the home, but the Eldridge Street minutes rarely mention women, discussing them mainly with regard to their status as widows or their purchase of cemetery plots. There were exceptions. In July 1903, Zlate Rivke Levy and Dina Wilensky "donated a beautiful white mantle for a Sefer Torah and a cover for the Reading Table"; in January 1913, a Mrs. Katz and a Mrs. Blum donated a new Torah.[36] In 1891 the khevre kedishe called for new women attendants; Yiddish books detailing the committee work of the khevre kedishe indicate that women in the congregation routinely assumed responsibilities and roles for the rituals surrounding preparation of the dead for burial. The indications are, then, that the Eldridge Street women engaged in continual charitable and ritual activities at the synagogue.

In 1907 the congregation amended its constitution to grant membership to widows, and it is reasonable to assume that it was Isaac Gellis's recent death and the communal standing of Sarah Gellis that prompted this first official recognition of women. Following this decision, widows who paid $10 in annual membership dues were now "considered members in good standing." Gellis became an active member; remarkably, a 1909 court document includes her signature where she joined twenty-one members, including her son Samuel, to attest that the merger of Kahal Adath Jeshurun with the Anshe Lubz congregation had been done with the congregation's knowledge and approval.[37] At the time of the court case, the congregation had well over two hundred members; the fact that Sarah was one of twenty-two representatives to sign this document underscores her status within the congregation. When she came to meetings or required the purchase of burial plots, the synagogue presidents always addressed her motions and requests.

Sarah Gellis's relative wealth enabled her to assume a more visible role than other women at the Eldridge Street Synagogue, but the constitutional change that enabled widows to become members affected women across the economic spectrum. Certainly, wealthy widows were a financial boon for a congregation, and evidence indicates that they were actively sought out. The widow Yakhe Itskovits paid a $125 entrance fee in 1918 in addition to her $8 membership dues, Frume Leah Berkowitz pledged the same amount in 1919, and Beyle Brand pledged $50 in 1921. New male members pledged $5, $20, and $25 in the same years. Yet between 1907 and 1918 most widows paid either $10 (for full membership) or $8 (for a seat) annually, and by 1918 the congregation had decided that members' widows did not have to pay dues at all, but one who kept her husband's seat paid $8.[38] In other words, less prosperous women members were also welcome.

Meanwhile, Jewish communal institutions, as opposed to congregations, granted immigrant women important leadership roles, opened up because of the enormous amount of work required to launch and operate new organizations. Rachel Hutkoff served on the board of directors of the Hebrew Sheltering Society's Ladies' Auxiliary in the early 1890s. The position was not just a nominal one, for the institution served tens of thousands of people a year (and one day served eight hundred people in its dining hall with only four people as paid staff), and, as the *New York Times* reported, "members spend their spare hours in performing the necessary labor at the institute." Upon Sarah Gellis's death in 1926, a Yiddish paper hailed her as the "famous East Side community do-er" who was an active member in many Jewish voluntary and charity societies.[39]

Formal and informal charity work and experience in communal endeavors was bound to affect the Eldridge Street congregation, which by the end of the second decade of the century was open to new forms of leadership. In late 1918, at the installation of a new rabbi, Avrohom Aharon Yudelovitch, women in attendance suggested the idea of a ladies' auxiliary. At the next general members session, in February 1919, a committee formed to "help the women" organize.[40] No doubt inspired by the movement to give women the right to vote—the Nineteenth Amendment became law the following year—the congregation decided to formalize the roles that women were playing behind the scenes. Members took an active interest in this auxiliary, and even though a woman served as president, a male member of the congregation took on the role of secretary; in the 1920s, Morris Dubrin, the sexton, assumed this role, and after his death in 1933, Morris Groob, the congregation's secretary, took over.

In addition to the holiday parties and the general work involved in maintaining a network of women and instilling in them the continued importance of

Breine and Morris Groob
Breine Groob was an active member of the Ladies' Auxiliary,
and her husband, Morris, served as secretary. Photograph courtesy
of Ester Fuchs.

the synagogue, the Ladies' Auxiliary regularly arranged Saturday evening meals, *melave malkes,* for the poor. Naomi Groob Fuchs recalls that her mother, Breine, and the other women in the organization prepared the meal in the synagogue's kitchen on Fridays: "They used to get together and cook, they used to have a good time." The women would set up tables downstairs and serve *tsholnt* (a stew with meat, potatoes, and other vegetables) or chicken soup at mealtime. Although the men who came for the meal were "Jewish hobos," the women served the finest foods: "Saturday night they would have a nice little party and sing songs."[41]

The work of the Ladies' Auxiliary combined an attachment to the Jewish calendar and its eternal observances with the more immediate concerns of maintaining the synagogue and the congregation. Its outreach work in the 1920s and 1930s proved crucial to the congregation's survival, after the National Origins

Act of 1924 drastically reduced the numbers of east European immigrants who could enter the United States, which diminished the prospects for a replenished congregation. As members left the Lower East Side for more upscale neighborhoods, the women's work became increasingly important as they strove to corral the resources and attention of those remaining in the neighborhood and retain the attachment of those who had moved away. In 1931 the president of the auxiliary, Freyde Walensky, created a poster for a Hanukah holiday party, an "evening of amusements" replete with "music [and] fine refreshments." Walensky stressed the importance of the gathering, requesting that none of the "sisters" miss the meeting. By 1935, the tone had become more urgent. President Sheyne Ester Israel considered the work of maintaining the congregation and the synagogue to be religious in nature, and in a Purim poster she urged the sisters to help out: "In the name of our holy synagogue I appeal to you, sisters, that you should return to your holy work for our synagogue. . . . With your participation in this work for the benefit of the synagogue, God will bless you . . . with long years and all that is good."[42]

In honor of the Ladies' Auxiliary's "holy work," in 1925 the congregation erected a handsome marble plaque on the sanctuary level that displayed the fifty names of the auxiliary's members. A twin plaque erected the same year in the same space listed the congregation's officers and trustees, but only ten members' names. A blank marble plaque adjoining it is still empty, suggesting that the congregation ran out of money before the list could be finished. The completed Ladies' Auxiliary plaque contains names like Freyde Walensky and Breine Groob, reminding us of the many roles that women played at the Eldridge Street Synagogue, whether they were quietly setting an example for their daughters in the balcony, preparing Saturday meals for the poor, or organizing holiday parties for the congregation.

In 1920, Jarmulowsky's bank was sold at a bankruptcy auction, a victim of neighborhood runs on the bank and the mismanagement of his sons, who had taken over the business upon his death.[43] Yet just around the corner, Jarmulowsky's first architectural contribution to New York's Orthodox Jewish community, the Eldridge Street Synagogue, endures. The appeals of the Ladies' Auxiliary to those who had once lived on the Lower East Side and prayed at the synagogue but who had moved to neighborhoods where the synagogue was far from view

Ladies' Auxiliary Plaque

The marble plaque installed on the northern wall of the sanctuary in 1925 to honor the Ladies' Auxiliary has "Ladies' Auxiliary" spelled out in Hebrew characters and the names of its fifty members. Photograph by Edward Cheng.

dominated the congregational agenda and work of both the men and the women. Members beckoned to the synagogue's diaspora to return, if not daily, then at least several times a year, to pray, study, or celebrate a *simkhe,* or joyful occasion. And just as the pioneer presidents had combined business expertise with piety to build and operate the synagogue, the men and women of the congregation called on the next generation to support the revered institution financially.

SEVEN

The Burning of the Mortgage

IN JANUARY 1930 the once-thriving congregation Mishkan Israel Anshe Suwalk sold its domed Byzantine synagogue on Forsyth Street, just around the corner from the Eldridge Street Synagogue. In the wake of the Jewish exodus to the boroughs and the stemming of the great tide of immigration from eastern Europe, Lower East Side synagogues were being sold and becoming churches. The congregation's loss of its synagogue, for years considered "one of the most prominent Jewish landmarks in the neighborhood," struck a local nerve. The Eldridge Street Synagogue's president, David Parnes, responded to the news of the Forsyth Synagogue's demise by summoning all members to a special meeting to remind them of their financial obligations. Should they neglect to pay their dues, Parnes warned, "we'll be in the same position as the Forsyth Shul."[1]

The Eldridge Street Synagogue was spared the fate of many of its former rivals. Its leadership provided ballast against the forces of decline by rallying both current members and those who had already moved on yet maintained an affection for their old synagogue. For years, the Eldridge Street alumni returned to the synagogue for High Holidays, weddings, and bar mitzvahs, and President Parnes and others understood that they could be counted on for help. The core congregation's efforts combined with the financial assistance of a larger circle of supporters were thus able to ensure the synagogue's survival even as attendance declined.[2]

When the Eldridge Street Synagogue opened, it competed with Beth Hamedrash Hagadol for prestige. Competition intensified as other synagogues appeared:

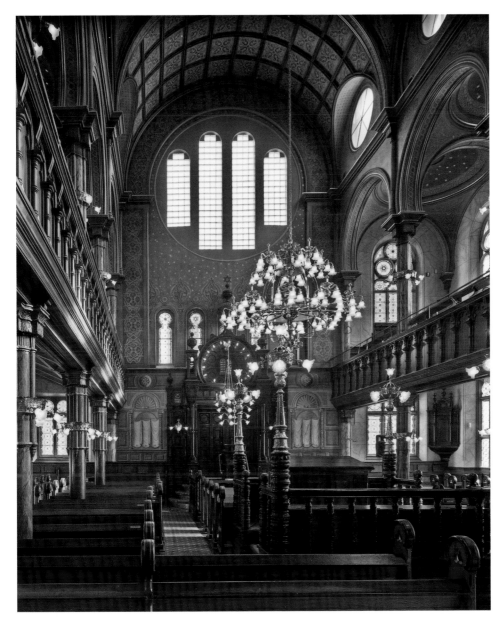

Glass Blocks

In 1938 a hurricane blew out sections of a circular stained-glass window above the ark. The congregation boarded up the window, hoping to replace it with stained glass in better financial times. In 1944 the congregation opted to add glass blocks in the shape of tablets—at $750, a more affordable option than stained glass. Photograph © 2007 by Kate Milford.

by the turn of the century new ones stood on nearby Forsyth and Pike Streets. Fifty years later, however, the Eldridge Street Synagogue congregation found itself vying not with neighborhood synagogues but with demographic shifts. In just a few decades, the vast majority of the Lower East Side's immigrant Jews had come and gone, reducing the population from a half million in 1910 to a quarter of a million in 1932 and creating new Jewish neighborhoods in the outer boroughs of the city.[3] Formerly successful methods of sparking membership, such as importing a great cantor or reducing membership rates, were insufficient, so in the 1920s and 1930s men like Parnes, Morris Groob, David Silver, and Morris Dubrin reached out to relocated members not just by updating the congregational address book but by developing a new message for them to hear. Drawing on the synagogue's history and reputation, the congregation cultivated a complex religious, familial, and communal identity that would appeal to Americanizing Jews, whether on the East Side or in Harlem, Brooklyn, or the Bronx.

Over the years the synagogue had given *tzedakah,* or charity, to neighborhood institutions through congregational fundraisers and presidential largess, contributions that had conferred upon it a certain status. Tzedakah was collected in the metal box affixed to the bes medresh wall. The design of the box, with six different slots representing six causes as well as the six days of the week on which tzedakah could be given, encouraged worshippers to contribute on a daily basis (Jewish law prohibits the handling of money on the Sabbath). The charitable activities pursued—from the repair of the library books to the support of Jewish settlements in Palestine—indicate the local to global issues that worshippers supported.

If the tzedakah box is a testament to the charity of members, it also symbolizes their consideration of needy Jewish causes throughout the world. In the 1920s and 1930s, even as members maintained their daily efforts to raise money for the local and international Jewish community, they drew upon the same notion of Jewish communal responsibility in engineering a campaign to enlist the financial support of New York Jewry for the benefit of their own synagogue.

The rich pioneer presidents of earlier generations were long gone, and now the congregation faced the Great Depression. Building maintenance had always devoured a fair share of earlier board presidents' time; now meeting minutes

Tzedakah Box
    This tzedakah box sat in the synagogue to enable congregants to obey the Jewish commandments
to help create a just world. Its unique design allowed for six different slots: one each for maintenance of the
building, the upkeep of cemeteries, and the proper care of religious books; two for Lower East Side institutions,
including a neighboring religious school and revolving charitable organizations; and one for a religious school
in Palestine. Photograph by Edward Cheng.

commonly noted items in need of repair, then that the necessary funds were not available. Attendees recall a "deteriorating" neighborhood and a "neglected" synagogue by the 1930s and 1940s, but they also remember a congregation that maintained its activities.[4] The khevre kedishe continued its work, for members and their children continued to buy plots in the congregation's cemeteries, and when they died, their families sought the society's care and services. The society kept its own budget, which was augmented with income from the annual November banquets. The congregation also orchestrated a Free Loan Society to help support congregants in straitened circumstances.

    To keep up with all the demands, core congregation members labored to raise funds and correspond with other members, inviting them to meetings and sending them bills. Letters show just how precarious the congregation's hold on their own synagogue had become: "We are very sorry to let you know that we are very much in need . . . we are $4000 behind in our budget. . . . We ask you dear

Free Loan Society Slip
In the 1920s and 1930s the congregation neglected the usual building repairs, saving money instead for a fund that would supply free loans to needy congregants.

brothers, how long will we need to suffer? . . . We can no longer go on with our work." A "Special Meeting Notice" from 1930 cited the more manageable sum of $800 to collect and begged for delinquent members to pay any money owed: "The steam is broken and we need to fix it, but money in the bank there is none, and our record books list a lot of debts [of members]. We can't send a collector, because that costs money . . . therefore, brothers and sisters, we ask you . . . to see to it that you send in your debts as soon as possible."⁵ Letters from the 1930s repeatedly refer to the fate of the Forsyth Street synagogue to motivate far-flung members to relieve the stress of the core congregants by supporting the synagogue.

Financial concerns and former presidents' financial wizardry notwithstanding, the core congregation as a whole supported leadership by a congregational rabbi, like Avraham Aharon Yudelovitch in the 1920s and Rabbi Yisroel "Idel" Idelson in the 1930s, men who combined scholarly credentials with oratorical skills. The continued value associated with scholarship shaped members' daily activities, too, inspiring regular study sessions. In 1922 a group in the congregation met daily to study chapters of the Mishnah and, in later years, Ein Ya'akov, a collection of legends from the Talmud that tell about the values, character, and experiences of rabbis. This group held a *siyum,* or banquet, in 1932, to celebrate their completion of Ein Ya'akov. The artwork adorning the group's record book, the invitation to the party — "Don't forget this great day that men have waited

גמ' משניות ועין יעקב

מקהל

עדת ישורין

עם אנשי ליובץ

12‎‏ 16‎‏ עלדרידז סט''

נתיסדה

שנת תרפ''ב

Cover of a Study Group Record Book

    In 1922 the congregation formed a study group to study Ein Ya'akov, and Morris Groob,
the congregation's secretary, designed the front cover of their record book.

for, for seven years!"—as well as a painting commissioned for the evening itself, featuring the group's rules and members, all show their pride of accomplishment. At the party Idelson delivered a speech, and the members' names were inscribed on the painting, along with the words *lizikhroyne oylem*, "to be remembered forever."[6]

Members of the congregation were loyal to the synagogue, fellow members, and Orthodox Judaism. As one frequent synagogue-goer recalled, Idelson's "very passionate" sermons "always dealt with being a Jew, remaining a Jew and observing," and this message filtered into the daily activities of the congregants. Naomi Groob Fuchs recalled that her father, Morris Groob, refused to collect the nominal payment offered to him in his position as secretary: "Fifty years he went to shul. Morning, afternoon, and night until he died. Besides being the secretary he was the head of the khevre kedishe. He would not take a vacation." When his children insisted that the parents go on vacation after forty years of marriage, he said, "'What if someone dies and I won't be around?' because he always said that would be the biggest *mitzvah* [commandment], that you take care of a dead person and they can't pay you back." Another member of the Ein Ya'akov club, Morris Dubrin, was also the *bal koyre* (Torah reader) and shames (sexton) of the congregation: "He devoted his whole life to the synagogue," leading services, officiating at weddings, and training boys for their bar mitzvahs. And Harry Smith, a trustee, spent hours at the synagogue and in the neighborhood each fall organizing and selling High Holidays tickets—the synagogue's major source of income—year after year. As his son Max explained, "This was my father's love, this shul. He loved this shul."[7]

Members like Dubrin, Groob, Parnes, Silver, and Smith established an extremely tight nucleus—almost like a family—that tackled such daily matters as study, prayer, mutual aid, and the administration of cemetery sales and funeral services. The nucleus also considered long-range goals and concerns and understood the need to place the Eldridge Street Synagogue on the agenda of the broader Jewish community. In doing so, they kept the substance—scholarship, family ties, and, of course, the preservation of the synagogue as a synagogue—paramount. However, when they reached out to the broader community by hosting a fiftieth-anniversary party, which involved placing advertisements, writing speeches, and

מקהל עדת ישורון עם אנשי לובז. · מקהל עדת ישורון עם אנשי לובז. · 1951-1952 תשי"ב · יאהרליכע חברה קדישא סעודה · יאהרליכע

Men at Table for a Banquet
Every November the congregation's burial society held a banquet (siyum) to raise money. This 1951 banquet was held in the bes medresh, with the longtime sexton David Parnes at the far right, Rabbi Kaidans third from the right, and Morris Groob, secretary, fifth from the right. Photograph courtesy of Ester Fuchs.

compiling a *50th Anniversary Souvenir Journal,* they adjusted the tone and emphasis of the message. At the banquet and in the *Journal,* the Eldridge Street Synagogue was hailed as a site for holy work, solace, and study and of beauty; mundane and worrisome matters such as broken steam heating, collection agencies, and threats of synagogue closure went unmentioned. In seeking wider support, they emphasized the synagogue's future and its place in New York Jewish history.

The celebration was held on December 28, 1934, at the Broadway Central Hotel, at Broadway and Third Street. That location, outside the Lower East Side boundaries, was presumably selected for the convenience of those coming from Midtown or the Bronx. Why was that date selected? It was the anniversary of neither the laying of the cornerstone (1886) nor the opening of the synagogue's doors to the public (1887); even an investigation into the more obscure founding dates of merger congregations fails to establish the logic for this ostensibly commemorative occasion. In fact, the need to raise funds and engage and augment members was so pressing that the congregation papered over the specifics of history in order to safeguard their own historic continuity. The goals were clear: to raise the money to pay off the mortgage and secure the synagogue's future as a Jewish institution. David Parnes's introductory speech raises the interrelated issues of geographic mobility, businesses, family, and identity: "The times change and we change with them. How many institutions founded fifty years ago are still around? And particularly among our people, who are always . . . changing their residences from downtown to uptown; from uptown to the Bronx, Brooklyn, Flatbush, etc., moving away, taking with them the best of the institutions that they founded. But, thank God, our synagogue, Kahal Adath Jeshurun Anshe Lubz, is [still here]." Parnes addressed both members and businessmen, suggesting that loyalty could be expressed in ways other than daily attendance. All Jews, members and nonmembers alike, could celebrate a synagogue that was "one of the most beautiful in New York, with a fine name and a fine popularity."

As the many speeches and the booklets full of advertisements attested, the congregation's future and, by extension, this place for "solace and spiritual guidance," were dependent on the contributions of businesses.[8] Undertakers, tailors, furriers, jewelers; hosiery and underwear retailers, and owners of monument stores, appetizer stores, and meat and poultry markets all supported the *50th Anniversary Souvenir Journal* by placing advertisements in it; they understood that their support helped them gain a good name among current and prospective customers who considered the synagogue a worthy cause. Professional advertisements placed by big businesses like Manischewitz ran alongside the business listings of core synagogue members; Hyman Foont, for example, paid to mention his pharmacy on nearby Market Street, and David Silver his hardware store on Essex Street. The advertisements of Louis Kram, who had left the congregation in 1909 to found the would-be branch in Harlem but who had continued to send contributions to the synagogue over the years, and Isaac Gellis, with his "Strictly Kosher Provisions," attested to the continued loyalty of old members and their children. By 1934 a good number of businesses advertising in the *Journal* were located in areas other than the Lower East Side — Midtown, Brooklyn, the Bronx, and New Jersey. Whether national or local, member or supporter, every advertiser

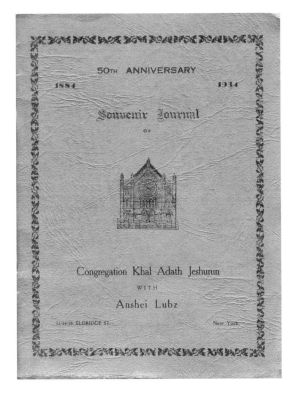

Golden Anniversary Journal
    In 1934 the congregation held a
fifty-year anniversary (three years early) and
started to raise the money needed to pay off
the mortgage on the synagogue.

was thanked in the *Journal* and, the committee wrote, "we highly recommend them to our members and friends."

The advertisements on behalf of businesses and donors were bracketed by speeches emphasizing the synagogue's historic and communal importance. Morris Groob's speech promoted the notion that the congregation's work should transcend matters of synagogue maintenance: "The last five years have brought vast, great events for the entire Jewish people, who are persecuted by strong forces from outside and by bitter poverty within. The Jewish masses have suffered, but with very, very great toil we have all successfully made it through. But our work is not yet complete. As great as the successes have been in the past, the duties for the future are just as great. A half-century has ended and a new half-century is beginning; we [enter it] filled with new energy."

While Groob's statement situated the synagogue and the congregation's work in the wider context of contemporary Jewry, Rabbi Idelson took a longer view. He reminded listeners and readers that the synagogue had been built from scratch — it was "among the first that were built in holiness from the foundation" — and that it had long provided "spiritual nourishment" for the Jewish people. Paying off the mortgage, he said, was a thread in the fabric of a larger Jewish destiny. Idelson referred to a belief in Jewish tradition that the Messiah's arrival would bring about the transplantation of Diaspora synagogues to Israel: Only after paying the mortgage "will we have a real celebration of the jubilee and we will go with the Synagogue to the Land of Israel." In this dramatic formulation, money sent to the Eldridge Street Synagogue would not just benefit a neighborhood shul but aid the congregation's efforts on behalf of the "greater struggle for Jewish interests," thereby securing its place in Jerusalem in Messianic times.

The congregation's struggle for Jewish interests had gained force during World War I, when it hired prominent rabbis as leaders, donated its space for Zionist mass meetings, and, most important, addressed the needs of Jewish communities in war-torn eastern Europe. In December 1915, for example, Shimon Lazerowitz, president of Kahal Adath Jeshurun and Anshe Lubz, organized a benefit concert at the Eldridge Street Synagogue to mourn the "Lubzer war sacrifices" and raise money for the struggling populace. The 1909 merger had brought a substantial number of members from the town of Lubz, now part of Belarus, into the Eldridge Street community. In a circular entitled "Help! Help!" Lazerowitz advocated a course of action: "Yes, terrible is the fate of our old home Lubz. And therefore we turn to you American Lubzers who find yourselves under the protection of America, and whose lives are calm and without fear of the Cossack and who enjoy all the freedoms. Help us! Give a little bread to the old and weak, or milk for the women to nurture their children! Don't let your parents, brothers, sisters, friends die a horrible death — from hunger."

Basic emotional ties bound all Lower East Side residents to their hometowns in eastern Europe. But wherever they came from, Jews in the United States shared a concern for Jews abroad and relief at being in America. Lazerowitz appealed to this broader community when he announced the December 29 concert in the *Morgn zhurnal*. The advertisement detailed the impressive array of speakers, including Alexander Harkavy, a prominent linguist, as well as choirs and cantors. It also made optimal use of the synagogue's seating system by offering four tiers of ticket prices, ranging from twenty-five cents to one dollar. The hope was to entice those in search of entertainment, those with a particular connection to Lubz, and those who simply needed an outlet for their grief over the pogroms and suffering in Europe. The concert would unite east European immigrants in New York and channel their funds to their brothers and sisters in eastern Europe.

The Eldridge Street Synagogue expanded its communal voice and attendance at events by cultivating a new role for its rabbis that melded scholarship with oratorical power. The congregation had always promoted scholarship and preaching, but separately, by hiring rabbis to study and guest preachers to preach. Various rules strictly defined the role of each functionary. Rabbis engaged to teach classes, such as Rabbi Yosef Eliyahu Fried, enjoyed the congregation's support and respect but did not assume leadership roles beyond the study sessions.[10] The record shows that the synagogue hired occasional speakers to grace the *amud*, or speaker's stand. In 1906 it decided to offer an annual contract to Moshe Mordecai Rivkind, who had been delivering sermons for several months. The contract required him to deliver sermons daily but restricted him from addressing "matters pertaining to the state, without permission from the president," and forbade him from using the title "rabbi of the shul." Although Rivkind was the face and voice of the congregation, the contract protected the congregation leadership's ultimate authority. Indeed, when Rivkind breached the contract later that year by using the title "Rabbi of Eldridge Street," he was investigated and dismissed.[11]

By the fall of 1918, when the congregation was courting Rabbi Avraham Aharon Yudelovitch, the situation had changed: the congregation clearly wanted him to assume the title Rabbi of Eldridge Street and to publicize his affiliation in the community. Yudelovitch took the position, forging a new and strengthened rabbinical role that he filled for close to a dozen years, until his death in 1930. By hiring Yudelovitch and then Idelson, who served from 1930 until his death in 1943, the congregation attracted Jews who came specifically for the rabbis' sermons and classes. Decades later, congregants recalled with pride the reputation of the rabbis at the Eldridge Street Synagogue in the 1920s and 1930s. A longtime congregant, Judge Paul Bookson, the grandson of the founder Kalmon Paston,

Rabbi Avraham Aharon Yudelovitch
Rabbi Yudelovitch served as the
congregation's rabbi from 1918 until 1930.

explained: "They were very highly learned rabbis. They were authors of books. Books on law. Jewish law. And their decisions were accepted and their works were studied, interpreted."[12]

That both Yudelovitch and Idelson had achieved a reputation through their scholarship, gaining them recognition in the Orthodox community on both sides of the ocean before they began their respective tenures at Eldridge Street, instantly brought an additional measure of fame to the synagogue that employed them. Yudelovitch, "recognized as one of the greatest scholars in the rabbinical spheres of America and Europe," "had played an enormous role in the traditional Jewish world." A graduate of the Volozhin Yeshiva in Lithuania, he had been ordained by the esteemed Rabbi Yom Tov Lipman and held rabbinical posts in eastern Europe, England, and the United States. He wrote scholarly works, including *Bet Av*, a collection of questions and answers, and books devoted to sermons. He viewed the United States as a "great field of activity for the spread of Torah and Jewishness, and with the energy of a young man . . . he threw himself into the work" when he arrived in New York in 1909, serving simultaneously as a congregational rabbi and as head of the Isaac Elchanan Yeshiva, forerunner to Yeshiva University, as well as head of national rabbinical consortiums. He was a "wonderful speaker," and his speeches "always captured his audience's hearts." Memories of Yudelovitch's sermons at Eldridge show that besides scholarship, he had a sophisticated understanding of the concerns and needs of the congregants: "He spoke very well. His sermons were very interesting. . . . Oh yes, he was a very worldly man, Yudelovitch." Yudelovitch also worked on behalf of Zionism and delivered fiery speeches at other synagogues and assemblies.[13]

Yudelovitch's renown enabled Kahal Adath Jeshurun and Anshe Lubz to draw people to the synagogue for special services, ceremonies, and speeches and even to ask other congregations and householders to help support his position on a permanent basis.[14] In May 1919, when a wave of riots against Jewish communities erupted in eastern Europe, New York's Jewish community reacted immediately, calling a meeting of ten thousand delegates to Madison Square Garden. Meanwhile, "thousands" of storekeepers and peddlers closed their businesses and pushcarts for a day of mourning, leaving placards to greet customers: "This store is closed to express our grief and sorrow over the massacres of Jews in Poland." Yiddish theaters held benefit performances, and Yiddish newspapers printed detailed reports on the events in Europe and summoned their readers to the protests in New York City. The Eldridge Street community sent delegates to the event at Madison Square Garden and, drawing on Yudelovitch's oratorical fame, invited the community at large to the Eldridge Street Synagogue. There they held a memorial for Rabbi Meir Simkhe, who had been killed in the most recent pogrom in Dvinsk, "shot in the middle of the street." The congregation featured their own rabbi in publicizing the event in the *Morgan zhurnal:* "The Rabbi from our synagogue, . . . Avraham Aharon Yudelovitch, the known preacher will eulogize. . . . All are welcome."[15]

When Yudelovitch died in 1930, the congregation wanted another rabbi known both for his scholarship and for his oratory. His successor, Idel Idelson, was considered among the "greatest rabbis in the country" and, like Yudelovitch, was very active in national rabbinical associations. He also directed efforts to aid

Rabbi Yisroel "Idel" Idelson
Rabbi Idelson served as the
congregation's rabbi from 1930 until 1943.
Photograph courtesy of Froma Zeitlin.

scholars in eastern Europe and "was among the first rabbis in the country to help in the development of Mizrachi," an Orthodox Zionist movement. Like Yudelovitch, he was celebrated for his ability to reach out to a wide audience: "He knew how to apply his great knowledge . . . to practical things." When the congregation hired him in 1930, his contract provided for sermons on Sabbaths and Sundays and study sessions on all other days of the week.[16]

Four years into his rabbinical position, Idelson captured the New York Jewish spotlight when he officiated at the funeral of Mendel Beilis. On July 9, 1934, four thousand Jews, directed by the Yiddish press to the "old Eldridge Street Synagogue . . . near Canal Street," arrived to mourn the loss of Beilis. The crowd could not be contained in the sanctuary. As many as a dozen policemen failed to establish order in the streets, and several women fainted in the commotion.[17]

Twenty years earlier, the Beilis trial in Russia had seized daily headlines in Yiddish and New York newspapers. The prosecution had accused Beilis of murdering a thirteen-year-old boy in Kiev in March 1911, giving as the motivation the alleged Jewish need for the blood of Christian children to make their Passover matzo. After two years Beilis was acquitted, causing a tremendous outpouring of joy in the world Jewish community. The overturning of the blood libel in Russia's courts boded well for the Jews—a sign that the new constitutional system could protect Jews from baseless medieval notions. The victory was seen as a triumph of modernity over medievalism, and Beilis became a modern hero. According to the *New York Times*, "His fellow-Jews always believed that his conduct during the next two years saved his countrymen from a pogrom."[18]

If part of the drama of the front-page story was the heroic way in which Mendel Beilis survived the blood libel accusation, gaining him worldwide acclaim in the second decade of the century, by the time of his death in 1934 as an unsuccessful insurance man, the tragedy was the Jewish community's failure to support and remember this man. As the extensive and detailed coverage in the Yiddish press following his death demonstrates, the immigrants and their children needed to be reminded about him. Although he had received a modicum of attention upon arriving in New York in 1922, he was unable to make a decent living, leading the Yiddish newspapers to concur in retrospect that Beilis somehow became a martyr after he was freed, when new horrors distracted Jews from his plight. An editorial in the *Tog* said: "He suffered on behalf of everyone, and should be remembered by everyone. But we forgot about him." No one more than Beilis exemplified Richard Wheatley's characterization of the immigrants as "fugitives from intolerable oppression and merciless cruelty." Yet he died poor and unsuccessful—the *Tog* claimed that "his personal life was full of sorrow, wandering, anguish, need and poverty"—unable to "harmonize" his "inner life with American currents of thought."[19]

Idelson's eulogy, quoted in the *Morgn zhurnal-tageblat*, touched on these points, occasionally moving both the crowd in the sanctuary and himself to tears. He evoked the heroic character of Beilis and the importance of his heroism to Jewish history. Idelson also stirred up a sense of collective guilt. A great martyr had survived a blood libel in Russia, and "in return the Jewish people forgot about him and he continued to suffer." The Jews could make amends, however, by remembering him. "As long as Jewry survives, so will his name and deeds." Idelson, in the name of the Jewish people, asked the departed for forgiveness and called for the creation of a fund for Beilis's widow and children. This fund was not for uptown or downtown Jews, socialists or the pious, to support, but one "that all Jews could support."[20]

Whereas the *Morgn zhurnal-tageblat* editorialized that "the Jewish people will remain indifferent and in several days he will remain only in the history of our sorrows," Idelson read the renewed interest in Beilis as a sign of hope and presented the occasion of his death as an opportunity for Jews of all backgrounds to affirm their sense of peoplehood. As the historian Arthur Goren has shown, in paying "tribute to the dead and to the past," immigrant funerals also addressed the present "by calling for rededication to the departed hero's way of life and goals." By recognizing, as did the newspapers, that such an event "made a great impression on all Jewish circles in New York," Idelson evoked Beilis's sacrifice on behalf of the Jewish people and called them to action on behalf of Jewish peoplehood.[21]

The fact that neither Beilis nor M. Kulok, the businessman who paid for the funeral, lived on the Lower East Side or were members of the Eldridge Street Synagogue spoke to the continued importance of the synagogue itself as a site for collective mourning and to the continued importance of its rabbi as a voice for the Jewish people. Idelson's goal—raising a fund to sustain Beilis's family—implied that a sense of peoplehood would be sustained not merely by reiterating and praising the values represented by the deceased but by affirming those values through financial contribution. Idelson knew how to bring his audiences to tears, and he directed the emotions and the heightened sense of collectivity evoked in each member of the audience by Beilis's trial and funeral toward an examination of his or her pocketbook as well as his or her soul.

Attachment to the Eldridge Street Synagogue was perpetuated not only by its communal significance but also through more intimate and often subtle family connections and associations, as Rabbi Idelson noted in the *Golden Anniversary Journal*. He knew from experience that synagogue attendance rose not only for funerals but also for bar mitzvahs and weddings. Indeed, many among the Eldridge Street diaspora found it difficult to imagine a family event not celebrated at the Eldridge Street Synagogue. As Idelson pointed out, "The children of the older members whose parents built the shul, and are no longer with us," are "bound to this shul due to the fact that they rest in the holy space of the shul, and are remembered four times a year by *haskores-neshomes* [prayers for deceased relatives recited on Jewish holidays]."

Oral histories contributed by members' children confirm the links that families had to the synagogue, which helped affirm their Jewish identity. As Rose Leibow Eisenberg recalled, her family's attachment to the synagogue proved so strong that even after they moved to the Bronx in 1914, they returned for the High Holidays: "When we lived in the Bronx we used to come down, I think for the first two or three years after we had moved, to go to shul Rosh Hashana and Yom Kippur. My parents wouldn't think of going anywhere else. Besides which, all the aunts and uncles [were there]. So those who lived on the East Side would put us up." Families also returned to mark rites of passage. Even after moving to the Bronx, Harry Smith sent his son, Max, back to the Lower East Side to study for his bar mitzvah with Morris Dubrin, whom Max recalled as a "terrific scholar," and Smith held the ceremony at Eldridge Street, too. The congregation presented Max, the son of an honored member, with a special ring, inscribed with the congregation's Hebrew name.[22]

Gilbert Lazarus, the grandson of Simon Lazerowitz, a president of the synagogue, recalled many details, including how "every family function in my childhood was held at the Eldridge Street Synagogue — every funeral, every wedding, every Bar Mitzvah." Even though his parents had moved to Harlem, his brother's bar mitzvah in 1919 was still held at their old synagogue, and the family went to great lengths to bring their new friends and neighbors from Harlem to Eldridge Street: "My father, who was quite Orthodox, did not want the guests to travel by any kind of vehicle. So he rented a whole floor or two at the Broadway Central Hotel, which was the only hotel down there. . . . So my father put up all the guests. They were invited to come down Friday afternoon and they held a small service in the hotel. Then they had dinner and whatever. The next morning, everybody had to traipse from Broadway to Eldridge Street." Most members and their children lacked the resources to rent a hotel floor for their guests, yet we can imagine that the desire to celebrate a family event at the Eldridge Street Synagogue, just as one's parents had done, was shared by families of lesser means. Lazarus reflected how the synagogue "became part of the fabric" of his grandfathers' and father's lives and how that led him to link his own identity to the synagogue: "To me, the Eldridge Street shul always represented a substantial part of my affiliation, even mentally, with Judaism, because my grandfathers and my father . . . they talked about it still as being part of their lives."[23]

Yet, as even the bearers of these memories concede, devotion to the synagogue could survive the passage of only several years. The Leibow family returned for the High Holidays, for the "first two or three years" after they moved. Gilbert Lazarus's older brother's bar mitzvah was held downtown at the synagogue, but by the time Gilbert himself had a bar mitzvah in 1925, the family had relocated once again, this time to the Bronx, where his father had become synagogue president, making it impossible for him to hold Gilbert's bar mitzvah ceremony anywhere other than their current congregation.

In other words, the period of time in which the Eldridge Street diaspora would act on its connections to the Eldridge Street Synagogue was, for most families, circumscribed. The core congregation seemed to grasp this dynamic early on, which may be why the congregation chose to have a fiftieth-anniversary celebration of the opening of the synagogue in the forty-seventh year; by shaving off three years, they jumpstarted the campaign to pay off the mortgage while they still had the attention of the members' children.

By October 1944, under the presidency of David Silver, the congregation had finally raised the $10,000 needed to pay off the mortgage. The deed record filed on October 16, 1944, records a membership of 150, a daily attendance of 25, and holiday attendance of 400, showing that the core congregation continued to pray and study at the synagogue and also worked at maintaining ties to the Eldridge Street diaspora. In turn, the members of the diaspora continued to identify with the synagogue, returning for High Holidays and special events and sending in dues. When the congregation officially celebrated the anniversary on March 18, 1945, members announced a free concert in the *Morgn zhurnal-tageblat* to welcome the entire community and promote the presence of great cantors, including Ben Zion Kapov Kagan. With the community as witness, they marked their ownership of the building with a ceremonial burning of the mortgage. The evening was remembered as a "swell affair."[24]

If in the heyday of the Eldridge Street Synagogue the East Side itself pro-

CONG. KAHAL ADAS JESHURUN
WITH ANSHEI LUBTZ
12-14-16 ELDRIDGE STREET

ADMISSION TICKET

to the DEDICATION
AND BURNING THE MORTGAGE
of OUR SYNAGOGUE,
SUNDAY EVE., MARCH 18, 1945, 7:00 P.M.

Paying Off the Mortgage

In the fall of 1944 the congregation paid off the mortgage. In March 1945 the entire Jewish community was invited to the synagogue for a celebration that featured refreshments, speeches, cantorial music, and the burning of the mortgage papers. Shown here are the invitation placed in the *Morgn zhurnal-tageblat*, an admission ticket, and the jar holding the fragments of the burned mortgage.

vided a sense of Jewish identity, by the 1940s it was the synagogue whose architecture and history spoke to a series of communal holidays, rites of passage, and transitions. And while daily events had scaled down considerably, requiring use of the grand sanctuary less and less, special communal and family events like the burning of the mortgage, High Holidays services, and an occasional bar mitzvah brought back all the traditional elements: a specially hired seasonal cantor, extended families, a crowded sanctuary, and a heightened sense of Jewish identity. It was, above all, the crowds in the synagogue and in the streets that offered a feeling of Jewish community lacking in the more diffuse borough neighborhoods and suburbs, as well as the Lower East Side of daily life. As Judge Paul Bookson recalled, "Emerging from the synagogue as the throngs would gather about in the middle of the street and on the opposite sidewalk . . . gave one a tremendous sense of identity and belonging to this vibrant and very numerous group."[25]

There is a certain irony in the congregation's achieving ownership of the synagogue right after World War II, just as more Jewish businesses and residents were leaving the neighborhood. As Judge Bookson said, "The real impact of the declining fortunes of Eldridge Street came . . . at the conclusion of that war, where people saw housing everywhere but in the cities." Benjamin Markowitz, the congregation's longtime shames, confirmed the decline: "And so the neighborhood changed and business moved up from the neighborhood to different locations . . . and mostly very little Jewish got left over in the neighborhood."[26]

For several more years, the congregation clung to the sanctuary for special events. But soon these became more infrequent, and even finding the requisite ten men for a minyan for weekday prayer sessions in the bes medresh became increasingly difficult, forcing congregants to venture to the nearby jewelry and tailor stores that lined Eldridge and Division Streets in search of worshippers. When such efforts failed, the congregation took to hiring neighborhood men or even yeshiva boys to make up the quorum. Unable to raise the funds to heat and maintain the sanctuary, at some point in the 1950s the congregation locked the sanctuary doors and held all their services in the bes medresh.

The tenacious congregation never missed a Sabbath service and perhaps, most important, never sold the building. Their loyalty to the synagogue kept it going until it was rediscovered in the 1970s by Gerard Wolfe, who founded the Friends of Eldridge Street and introduced visitors to the synagogue on his walking tours. Then Roberta Brandes Gratz and William Josephson formed the Eldridge Street Project, paving the way for a creative restoration that not only salvaged the building but returned it to its 1887 glory. The congregation continues to pray and worship at the Eldridge Street Synagogue on the Sabbath and Jewish holidays, while on weekdays and Sundays, schoolchildren and tourists of all ages and backgrounds come to learn about the immigrant founders and their children and the challenges they encountered in creating and maintaining a space for Orthodox Jewish religious life in the United States.

Notes

CHAPTER ONE. A LANDMARK SYNAGOGUE

1. Wolfe, *Synagogues of the Lower East Side;* Mendelsohn, *Lower East Side Remembered and Revisited;* "A New East Side Synagogue," *New York Herald,* September 5, 1887 (quotation).

2. According to the National Historic Landmark Nomination report prepared for the Eldridge Street Synagogue, the first east European synagogue to be built as a synagogue was actually Beth Israel in Rochester, New York. However, the report notes that this synagogue, built in five months, was a modest structure, described as "plain but good looking, without decoration." Renee Newman, Maria Schlanger, and Amy E. Waterman, National Historic Landmark Nomination, The Eldridge Street Synagogue, U.S. Department of the Interior, National Park Services, 1996. See also Abraham Karp, "An East European Congregation on American Soil: Beth Israel, Rochester," in Bertram Wallace Korn, ed., *A Bicentennial Festschrift for Jacob Rader Marcus* (New York: Ktav Pub. House, 1976), pp. 263–302.

3. Richard Wheatley, "The Jews in New York," *Century Magazine,* January 1892, p. 330.

4. The quotation is from remarks made by Roberta Brandes Gratz at the Eldridge Street Project's Landmark Celebration, 1996. Gerard Wolfe's walking tours of the neighborhood and his subsequent founding of the Friends of Eldridge Street introduced visitors to the Eldridge Street Synagogue and raised money for heating the synagogue in the 1970s. Wolfe's work brought the synagogue to the attention of the Landmarks Preservation Commission of the City of New York in December 1979. Wolfe's tours brought William Josephson to the Eldridge Street Synagogue, who in turn brought Roberta Brandes Gratz. Wolfe's 1971 rediscovery of the synagogue is

recounted in Wolfe, *Synagogues of the Lower East Side*, pp. 43–45; "Restoration," *New Yorker*, September 26, 1988; and "Transcript of the Remarks Made by Professor Gerard R. Wolfe at the Meeting of the Landmarks Preservation Commission," December 11, 1979, Collection of the Museum at Eldridge Street. Key to the interpretive development of the Eldridge Street Project were Richard Rabinowitz, of the American History Workshop, and Amy E. Waterman, executive director of the Eldridge Street Project from 1992 to 2007. For the nomination of the synagogue for landmark status, see Newman, Schlanger, and Waterman, National Historic Landmark Nomination.

5. Jill Gotthelf was the architect of the restoration for eighteen years; Walter Sedovic joined Gotthelf in 2000.

6. Hertzberg, "Treifene Medinah," pp. 7–30; Sarna, *American Judaism*, pp. 154–156. In general, Yiddish words are transliterated according to the YIVO system of romanization. English words of Yiddish or Hebrew origin found in *Merriam-Webster's Collegiate Dictionary* are, for the most part, spelled as they are in the dictionary. When quoting a text, I have used the given rendering. When the official name of an organization has a romanization that differs from YIVO's, I have used the organization's spelling of its name.

7. Rischin, *Promised City*, pp. 23–26 (quotation); Kahan, "Economic Problems"; Kuznets, "Immigration of Russian Jews"; Sarna, *American Judaism*, pp. 151–154; Diner, *Lower East Side Memories*, p. 35.

8. Sarna, *American Judaism*; Gurock, *American Jewish Orthodoxy*; Goren, *New York Jews*.

9. Weinberger, *People Walk on Their Heads*, p. 41; Ish Yemini [Adolph Benjamin], "Dedication of Congregation Adath Jeshurun," *American Hebrew*, September 9, 1887; Der rov hakolel?" *Di arbeter tseytung*, March 23, 1891. See also Michels, *Fire in Their Hearts*, p. 14.

10. See, for example, the contracts for preachers hired in the early 1900s. Minutes of the Eldridge Street Synagogue (henceforth ESS Minutes), April 12, 1906; April 7, 1907. The minutes are in the Collection of the Museum at Eldridge Street.

11. ESS Minutes, May 11, 1919. On immigrants' observance of the Sabbath, see Anne Polland, "Sacredness of the Family: New York's Immigrant Jews and Their Religion, 1890–1930," Ph.D diss., Columbia University, 2004.

12. Karp, "New York Chooses a Chief Rabbi," p. 191 (quotation); Ledger, 1888–1909, page titled "Subscription List of the Association of Hebrew Orthodox Congregations," Congregation Kahal Adath Yeshurun with Anshe Lubitz (New York, NY) records, American Jewish Historical Society (henceforth Congregation, AJHS), RG

I-10, Box 3. On the experiment in importing a shared rabbi, see Karp, "New York Chooses a Chief Rabbi."

13. ESS Minutes, November 4, 1900.

14. "Anti-Vice Mass Meeting," *New York Times*, April 23, 1900 (quotation). Examples of organizations supported by the congregation include Mount Sinai Hospital, Yeshiva Etz Chaim, Volozhin Yeshiva, Hospital in Tiberias, Machzike Talmud Torah, Lebanon Hospital, Montefiore Talmud Torah, Yeshiva of Eishishok, Hakhnoses Orkhim Society, Beth Israel Society, United Hebrew Charity, Bnos Ya'akov, Gan Yeladim, Malbish Arumim, Maskil al Dal, Tomchei Shabbos, and Rabbi Jacob Joseph Yeshiva. ESS Minutes, 1890–1916.

15. ESS Minutes, April 30, 1889; "Meetings in Synagogues," *New York Times*, September 20, 1901. For the flag see ESS Minutes, June 23, 1918. For assemblies see ESS Minutes, May 18, 1919; *Morgn zhurnal*, May 19, 1919.

16. Congregation Kahal Adath Jeshurun with Anshe Lubz, Constitution, June 22, 1913, Collection of the Museum at Eldridge Street.

17. Congregation Kahal Adath Jeshurun with Anshe Lubz, *50th Anniversary Souvenir Journal*, 1934, Collection of the Museum at Eldridge Street; Oral history interviews of Naomi Groob Fuchs, conducted by Ruth Abram, 1986; of Gussie Dubrin, conducted by Judy Tenney, 1991; of Gilbert Lazarus, conducted by Roberta Brandes Gratz, 1991; of Max Smith, conducted by Renee Newman, 1996; and of Lillian Rabinowitz Fried, conducted by Judy Tenney, 1991, all in the Collection of the Museum at Eldridge Street.

CHAPTER TWO. LAYING THE CORNERSTONE

1. Ledger, Congregation, AJHS, RG I-10, Box 17, p. 5. For an analysis of nineteenth-century synagogue cornerstone events and the way they blended Jewish religious objects and American civic ceremonials, see Goren, "Public Ceremonies Defining Central Synagogue," pp. 41–74.

2. "Kahal Adas Yeshurun," *Yidishe gazeten*, November 12, 1886.

3. For the congregants' recollections see Eisenstein, "History." On the central European wave of Jewish migration, see Diner, *Time for Gathering*. On the central European Jewish experience in New York City, see Grinstein, *Rise of the Jewish Community*. On Beth Hamedrash see Eisenstein, "History"; Eisenstein, *Ozar Zikhronothai*, p. 247; Grinstein, *Rise of the Jewish Community*, p. 474.

4. The founders of Beth Hamedrash included Abraham Joseph Ash, Abba Baum, Abraham Benjamin, Israel Cohen, Leib Cohen, Eliah Greenstein, David Lasky, Benjamin Lichtenstein, Judah Middleman, Feibel Phillips, Baruch Rothschild, Joshua Roth-

stein, plus Jerahemiel Chuck, Wolf Cohen, Nyman Harris, Samuel Hillel Isaacs, Abraham Levy, Jacob Levy, Isidor Raphall, Leibel Ratzker, Abraham Rener, and Tobias Schwartz. The first twelve were the original founders, and the rest joined shortly thereafter. Eisenstein, "History," p. 64. On the Pearl Street meeting place see Anbinder, *Five Points*, p. 243. On synagogues in 1860 see Grinstein, *Rise of the Jewish Community*, pp. 39–57.

5. When the congregation moved to Pearl and Center Streets, they elected a president (first Isidor Raphall and later Joshua Rothstein) and started paying their rabbi and sexton. Eisensten, "History," p. 65.

6. Grinstein, *Rise of the Jewish Community*, pp. 12 (quotation), 253, 263, 412.

7. Eisenstein, "History," p. 66. The year on the congregation's stamp is 1856, the year the congregation moved to 78 Allen Street. The congregation formally incorporated on June 16, 1858. Record of Religious Incorporations, Volume II, #2RC-P204, Office of the City Register.

8. Krinsky, *Synagogues of Europe*, p. 8 (quotation); official responsa from Mata'e Moshe (Moses Aaronsohn) and Yosef Natanson, as summarized in Eisenstein, *Ozar Zikhronothai*, p. 341.

9. Congregation Kahal Adath Jeshurun with Anshe Lubz, Constitution, June 22, 1913, Collection of the Museum at Eldridge Street [Hebrew section].

10. Hasia Diner, "Looking for Laity in All the Right (and Wrong) Places: The Place of the Laity in the History of American Judaism," in Wertheimer, *Jewish Religious Leadership*. Moses Aaronsohn, upon his arrival in New York in 1862, served as the rabbi of Beth Hamedrash. The earliest extant ledger, from 1882 to 1887, indicates that the Allen Street congregation hired rabbis/preachers throughout this period. Ledger, 1882–1887, Congregation, AJHS, RG I-10, Box 1; Glogower, "Responsa Literature," p. 263.

11. "The Trustees of the Congregation Beth Hamedrash against the Manhattan Railway Company," New York Supreme Court Law Judgment, 1899-399, New York City Division of Old Records; Minda Novek, Richard Rabinowitz, and Amy Waterman, "Historical Detective Work," American History Workshop, 1991.

12. "Dedicating a Synagogue," *New York Times*, August 17, 1885; Ish Yemini [Adolph Benjamin], "Dedication of Congregation Adath Jeshurun," *American Hebrew*, September 9, 1887 (quotation); Ledger, Congregation, AJHS, RG I-10, Box 17; see also "Recorded Real Estate Transfers," *New York Times*, December 2, 1886. The name was officially changed on April 22, 1890. Application to Change Corporate Name, "The Trustees of Congregation Beth Hamedrash" to "Kahal Adath Jeshurun," #RC 25, New York County Clerk, Change of Names of Religious Organizations, New

York Court of Common Pleas. The 1890 "Application to Change Corporate Name" papers do not provide English translations. On the translation and court documents see Kahal Adath Jeshurun em Anshe Lubtz Incorporation Certificate, New York Supreme Court Case 5352-1909C, Special Term, April 8, 1909.

13. New York City Department of Buildings, Application for the Erection of Buildings, No. 1266/86; Amendment, September 16, 1886; and Final Report of Inspection, September 30, 1887, NYC Municipal Archives.

14. On the Moorish style as applied to synagogues see Krinsky, *Synagogues of Europe;* Wischnitzer, *Synagogue Architecture in the United States.*

15. Stewart, "Programme for Preservation," p. 12 (quotation); Kaufman, *Shul with a Pool,* p. 183.

16. "Dedicating a Synagogue," *New York Times,* August 17, 1885.

17. Weinberger, *People Walk on Their Heads,* p.105.

18. A September 2, 1887, advertisement announced Feinsilber's move to 41 Eldridge; an August 20, 1886, advertisement indicates that he had been located at 79 Bayard Street. Both advertisements appeared in the *Yidishe gazeten.*

19. The Natelsons' advertisement was run in the *Yidishe gazeten* as early as September 24, 1886, and ran through the season. I am grateful to Celia Bergoffen for calling my attention to this advertisement and to Shmuel Pultman, who initially called Bergoffen's attention to it. In the eighteenth and nineteenth centuries it was customary in New York synagogues for the wife of the sexton to manage the mikvah. Grinstein, *Rise of the Jewish Community,* pp. 253, 298.

20. Celia Bergoffen, "The Proprietery Baths and Possible Mikvah at 5 Allen Street," March 31, 1997, p. 25, Collection of the Museum at Eldridge Street; Tax Photos Collection, Block 293, Lot 19, Municipal Archives, New York City.

21. The mikvah at 78 Allen Street may have been the oldest in New York remaining in continuous use, but the first mikvah built in New York was in fact Shearith Israel's, in 1759; the congregation moved uptown in 1833. Grinstein, *Rise of the Jewish Community,* pp. 297–298. The Natelsons' advertisement appeared in the *Yidishe gazeten,* October 14, 1887. The four mikvahs advertising between 1886 and 1887 in the *Yidishe gazeten* include the ones at 78 Allen, 5 Allen, 80 Forsyth (the mikvah of Kol Israel Anshe Polin), all of which advertised on October 14, 1887, and the one at 99 Attorney Street (the mikvah of Anshe Sfard Ostreich-Ungarin), called the "most kosher mikvah in all of New York," whose advertisement appeared on August 20, 1886. A December 7, 1884, article in the *New York Daily Tribune* lists fifteen mikvahs attached to synagogues.

22. Heinze, *Adapting to Abundance,* p. 58. Visits to a mikvah are considered acts of

purification. Women are required to visit the mikvah before marriage and then on a monthly basis, after menstruation. The Mishnah, the third-century collection of Jewish oral laws, provides the specifications for the pools, and Maimonides' twelfth-century commentaries and the sixteenth-century Shulkhan Arukh elaborate on them. Customarily, rabbis, who know Jewish law, supervise the construction. The importance of the rabbi's role with regard to late-nineteenth-century mikvahs in New York is evidenced by mikvah advertisements, each of which posts the various rabbinical certifications they received. Moses Weinberger noted that the certifying rabbis visited the mikvah before it opened but did not check to ensure that the mikvah was properly maintained or that the practices at the mikvah remained ritually correct. Weinberger, *People Walk on Their Heads*, p. 117.

23. Ibid., p. 72; Peter Wiernik, "Idishkeyt in amerike," *Minikes' Yom Tov Bleter*, April 1906, p. 21.

CHAPTER THREE. OPENING DAY

1. *Yidishe gazeten*, September 2, 1887 ("thousands"); "Cong. Adath Jeshurun," *American Hebrew*, September 9, 1887 ("immense").
2. Sarna, *American Judaism*, p. 177.
3. Ledger, Congregation, AJHS, RG I-10, Box 17; *Yidishe gazeten*, September 2, 1887.
4. Sarna, *American Judaism*, p. 88.
5. Ibid., pp. 149, 150.
6. Mi Yodea, "New York," *American Israelite*, September 16, 1887.
7. Leon Jick, "The Reform Synagogue," in Wertheimer, *American Synagogue*, p. 93.
8. Mi Yodea, "New York."
9. Ish Yemini [Adolph Benjamin], "Dedication of Congregation Adath Jeshurun," *American Hebrew*, September 9, 1887. Adolph Benjamin was born in Lithuania in 1848 and in 1882 came to New York, where he worked to protect Jewish children from Christian missionary influence. Marcus, *Concise Dictionary of American Jewish Biography*, p. 180.
10. "More Rabbis Needed," *American Hebrew*, September 23, 1887.
11. *Jewish Messenger*, October 14, 1887.
12. *Yidishe gazeten*, September 16, 1887.
13. Kasriel Sarasohn, "Kahal Adas Yeshurun," *Yidishe gazeten*, September 16, 1887. On September 17 the *Jewish Messenger* also noted the lack of a rabbi.
14. Throughout the congregation's tenure on Allen Street, monthly payments indicate that they were paying a rabbi/preacher. Ledger, 1882–1887, Congregation, AJHS,

RG I-10, Box 1. On the salary and the contract see Karp, "New York Chooses a Chief Rabbi," p. 191.

15. Richard Wheatley, "The Jews in New York," *Century Magazine*, January 1892, p. 324 ("currents"); Yemini [Benjamin], "Dedication of Congregation Adath Jeshurun." On Orthodox Judaism and American life, see Gurock, *American Jewish Orthodoxy in Historical Perspective;* Joselit, *New York's Jewish Jews;* Sarna, *American Judaism.* On the Eldridge Street Synagogue's involvement in Jewish communal organizations such as the Orthodox Union, see "The Conference of the Jews," *New York Times,* June 10, 1898; "Orthodox Jews Meet," *New York Times,* December 31, 1900; "Orthodox Jews Resist Kehillah," *New York Times,* April 11, 1913.

16. Stewart, "Programme for Preservation," pp. 3–4.

17. Kamil and Wakin, *Big Onion Guide to New York City,* p. 41. On tenement housing on the Lower East Side, see Dolkart, *Biography of a Tenement House.*

18. *American Magazine,* November 1888, quoted in Rischin, *Promised City,* p. 82 ("prison-like"); Wolfe, *Synagogues of the Lower East Side,* p. 27 ("hastily").

19. Gurock, *American Jewish Orthodoxy in Historical Perspective,* p. 256; Oral history interview of Gussie Dubrin, conducted by Judy Tenney, 1991, Collection of the Museum at Eldridge Street; Yezierska, *Hungry Hearts,* p. 255.

20. "Tiny Places of Worship: The Humble Synagogues of the Poorer East Side," *New York Daily Tribune,* February 16, 1896 ("Scores"); "Four Killed, Many Hurt," *New York Times,* September 24, 1892 (Ludlow Street); Edward Steiner, "The Russian and Polish Jew in New York," *Outlook,* November 1, 1902 ("halls").

21. E. S. Martin, "East Side Considerations," *Harper's New Monthly Magazine,* May 1898, p. 858; David Kaufman, "Constructions of Memory: The Synagogues of the Lower East Side," in Diner, Shandler, Wenger, *Remembering the Lower East Side,* p. 119.

CHAPTER FOUR. MUSIC AND MONEY

1. *Yidishe gazeten,* September 16, 1887; Ledger, 1882–1887, Congregation, AJHS, RG I-10, Box 1.

2. Weinberger, *People Walk on Their Heads,* p. 99; Slobin, *Chosen Voices,* p. 52 (Weinshel); *Yidishe gazeten,* July 13, 1886 (Cooper, Michalovsky). See also Wiernik, *History of the Jews in America,* p. 284.

3. Slobin, *Chosen Voices,* p. 52. Minkowsky mentions that by the summer of 1887, Cooper had left Vilna for New York, which was why that community was then courting Minkowsky. Pinhas Minkowsky, "Mi-sefer hayai," *Reshumot* (Tel Aviv: Davir, 1930), p. 99.

4. Eisenstein, "History," p. 74. Eisenstein writes that the Eldridge Street congregation brought Minkowsky over in 1886 and that that prompted Beth Hamedrash Hagadol to bring over Michalovsky. However, in *Oẓar Zikronothai*, Eisenstein correctly notes the date of Minkowsky's arrival as September 16, 1887.

5. Sarna, introduction to Weinberger, *People Walk on Their Heads*, p. 13; Slobin, *Chosen Voices*, p. 52; Wiernik, *History of the Jews in America*, pp. 283–284.

6. Pinhas Minkowsky, "Otobiografye," in Jewish Ministers and Cantors Association of America, *Di geshikhte fun khaẓones* (New York: Pinski-Massel, 1924), p. 85.

7. Mi Yodea, *American Israelite*, August 19, 1887 (quotation); Kessner, *Golden Door*, p. 66.

8. Sarna, *American Judaism*, p. 13.

9. Mi Yodea, *American Israelite*, August 19, 1887 ("achieve"); *Yidishe gaẓeten*, September 2, 1887 ("world-famous").

10. Minkowsky, "Otobiografye," p. 85.

11. ESS Minutes, December 7, 1890; January 11, 1891; November 15, 1891.

12. Letter to Kahal Adath Jeshurun from Cantor Pinhas Minkowsky, December 13, 1891, translated by Sylvia Tuchman and Rabbi Armand Friedman, Collection of the Museum at Eldridge Street; Eisenstein, *Oẓar Zikhronotai*, pp. 57–58.

13. ESS Minutes, May 1, 1892.

14. Minkowsky, "Otobiografye," p. 86.

15. Weinshel is quoted in Slobin, *Chosen Voices*, p. 53. See also Wiernik, *History of the Jews in America*, p. 284; Sarna, *American Judaism*, p. 14; Slobin, *Chosen Voices*, p. 56.

16. ESS Minutes, July 30, 1892; October 16, 1892.

17. Letter to Congregants from President Shimon Lazerowitz and Secretary Yehuda Leib Gribetz, August 1913, Congregation, AJHS, RG I-10, Box 2.

18. Jacob Pfeffer, "Idishkeyt," *Morgn ẓhurnal*, September 18 and 21, 1908.

19. Adina Klein, "Minkowsky, Odessa and Modernization: A Hazzan's Response to Reform" (Master's thesis, Cantors' Institute, Jewish Theological Seminary, 1992), p. 8; Zaludkowski, *Kultur-treger*, p. 202.

20. Efroyim Kaplan, "The Appearance of Our Shuls," *Morgn ẓhurnal*, September 19, 1912. See also Kaplan, "Elul in Amerike," *Morgn ẓhurnal*, September 15, 1910.

21. Ida Rothman Feely, "Growing Up in the East Side of New York City," Family Reminiscences, Small Collections 3365, American Jewish Archives.

22. Slobin, *Tenement Songs*, pp. 19, 169; "Farvos a sakh barimter khazonim farlozen itst amerike," *Forverts*, July 8, 1933. For stories about cantors, see, for example, letters in *Forverts* on September 16 and September 28, 1902.

23. Slobin, *Chosen Voices*, p. 60.

24. "Pinhas Minkowsky," *Tageblat*, January 21, 1924.

25. Ibid.

26. "Pinhas Minkowsky," *Di idishe muzikalishe velt* (New York: Lazarus Monfrid, 1923), p. 10.

CHAPTER FIVE. *E PLURIBUS UNUM*

1. "Froyen agitiren in di shulen forn kheyrem," *Forverts*, May 18, 1902; Hyman, "Immigrant Women and Consumer Protest."

2. "Froyen agitiren."

3. "Tiny Places of Worship: The Humble Synagogues of the Poorer East Side," *New York Daily Tribune*, February 6, 1896; Louis Lipsky, "Religious Life," in Bernheimer, *Russian Jew in America*, p. 40.

4. Richard Wheatley, "The Jews in New York," *Century Magazine*, January 1892, pp. 329–330.

5. Ibid., p. 330.

6. Kaufman, *Shul with a Pool*, p. 170. Though many of these landsmanshaften—geographically based associations—adopted members from places besides their own home town or region, especially in the case of a son-in-law, the impetus for forming an association and the primary mode of identification was nevertheless with the European town. Soyer, *Jewish Immigrant Associations and American Identity*.

7. Ledger, Congregation, AJHS, RG I-10, Box 17 (quotation). Although an obituary for Max or "Note" Lubetkin says that the Vizaner congregation formed in 1879, Holkhe Yosher Vizaner's official stamp on the incorporation deed ceding lots 12 and 14 Eldridge Street to "Kol Adas Jeshurun" indicates the congregation's founding date as 1870. "Congregation Holche Josher Wizaner to Congregation Kol Adas Jeshurun, Deed, May 25, 1886; "Mister Max Lubetkin," *Morgn zhurnal*, March 6, 1919. On synagogues in this period in New York, see Grinstein, *Rise of the Jewish Community*. On Kahal Adath Jeshurun in particular, see Gurock, "Stage," p. 9.

8. Oral history interview of Naomi Groob Fuchs, conducted by Ruth Abram and Joan Bieter, June 16, 1986, Collection of the Museum at Eldridge Street.

9. Gurock, "Stage," p. 10 ("rich man's"). On prices see Hapgood, *Spirit of the Ghetto*, p. 115. That tickets were not normally required is suggested by the special notices in the minutes when particular holidays or Sabbaths required tickets. ESS Minutes, February 25, 1891.

10. ESS Minutes, March 27, 1898 (quotation). Thirty percent paid in the $30–$40 range in 1897–1898; 27 percent paid in the $20–$30 range; 22 percent paid in the $10–$20 range; 15 percent paid in the $40–$50 range; 7 percent paid in the $50–$60 range. Ledger,

1898, Congregation, AJHS, RG I-10, Box 9; Congregation Kahal Adath Jeshurun with Anshe Lubz, Constitution, June 22, 1913, Collection of the Museum at Eldridge Street.

11. A renter could enjoy all the benefits for a yearly sum of $10, which was also divided into payments. ESS Minutes, May 10, 1891.

12. ESS Minutes, February 14, 1892.

13. ESS Minutes, January 5, 1892.

14. ESS Minutes, November 10, 1901.

15. ESS Minutes, May 10, 1891.

16. Congregation Kahal Adath Yeshurun with Anshe Lubz, Constitution.

17. Oral history interview of Yossi Paston, conducted by Beth Edberg, 1991, Collection of the Museum at Eldridge Street; ESS Minutes, August 28, 1906. For example, the Radishkovitser Lodge Order Brith Abraham rented the lower level for $200 for the holiday. ESS Minutes, August 26, 1902.

18. Edward Steiner, "The Russian and Polish Jew in New York," *Outlook*, November 1, 1902 ("everybody goes"); "Lack of Synagogue Accommodations," *American Hebrew*, August 23, 1912 ("mushroom synagogues"); "The Season of Piety" (editorial), *Morgn zhurnal*, September 21, 1908; *New York Post*, September 15, 1897, quoted in Rudolf Glanz, "Jewish Social Conditions as Seen by the Muckrakers," *YIVO Annual*, 9 (1954): 327 ("net proceeds"). That everyone attended Days of Awe services was reported in "Phases of Yom Kippur: Odd Mingling of Ancient and Modern in Synagogue Congregations," *New York Daily Tribune*, October 13, 1902. The reporter was struck by the fact that both young and old men practiced these rites. For a gray-haired, bearded man to engage in such practices seemed fitting, but to see "a young man, in a Derby hat of this season's vintage, and very smart as to collar and tie, beating his breast as he prayed, . . . produced a curious sensation." Scholars and contemporary observers have often interpreted failure to attend church regularly as a wholesale abandonment of religion. Scholars of religious life and popular religion have challenged these assessments, arguing that the practices — usually holidays and life-cycle events — kept and adapted can be used to indicate what aspects of religious life were held sacred. Orsi, *Madonna of 115th Street;* Williams, "Urban Popular Religion."

19. Kahal Adath Jeshurun em Anshe Lubtz Incorporation Certificate, New York Supreme Court Case 5352-1909C, Special Term, April 8, 1909, p. 7; ESS Minutes, August 1, 1904 ("tickets printed"); Gurock, "Orthodox Synagogue," p. 48.

20. Jonathan Sarna, "The Debate over Mixed Seating in the American Synagogue," in Wertheimer, *American Synagogue;* Seat Contract, 1887, for L. Matlawsky, secretary,

Collection of the Museum at Eldridge Street (quotation). The separation of men and women in public worship comes from a Talmudic description of a women's section in the Ancient Temple in Jerusalem. Goldman, *Beyond the Synagogue Gallery*, p.5.

21. Mi Yodea, *American Israelite*, September 16, 1887.

22. A visiting Christian minister in 1812, quoted in Goldman, *Beyond the Synagogue Gallery*, p. 41 ("breast-work"); Goldman, *Beyond the Synagogue Gallery*, p. 46 ("close front"). The change in the women's balcony had to do more with Americanization than with a change in religious ideology. Gurock, *American Jewish Orthodoxy in Historical Perspective;* Jick, *Americanization of the Synagogue;* Prell, *Prayer and Community;* Sarna, *American Judaism.*

23. Wheatley, "Jews in New York," pp. 329–330.

24. Oral history interview of Miriam Aaron, conducted by Renee Newman, 1995, Collection of the Museum at Eldridge Street.

25. Oral history interview of Gussie Dubrin, conducted by Judy Tenney, 1991; of Rose Eisenberg, conducted by Roberta Brandes Gratz, 1991; and of Lillian Rabinowitz Fried, conducted by Judy Tenney, 1991, all in the Collection of the Museum at Eldridge Street.

26. On decorum and the American Synagogue, see Jick, *Americanization of the Synagogue;* Wertheimer, *American Synagogue;* Prell, *Community and Prayer;* Sarna, *American Judaism.* On the Eldridge Street Synagogue in particular, see Gurock, "Stage,"

27. The constitution empowered the congregation's twelve trustees "to fine members for disobedience of their orders." A first offense cost the errant congregant twenty-five cents; the second, fifty cents. At that point, if the chatty congregant failed to oblige, the trustee might report him to the president of the congregation, whose job description included maintenance of "order and decorum." Congregation Kahal Adath Jeshurun with Anshe Lubz, Constitution.

28. Grinstein, *Rise of the Jewish Community*, p. 266.

29. Mordecai Kaplan, *Communings of the Spirit: The Journals of Mordecai M. Kaplan,* vol. 1: *1913–1934,* ed. Mel Scult (Detroit, MI: Wayne State University Press, 2001), p. 274.

30. Ibid., pp. 273–274.

31. Congregation Kahal Adath Jeshurun with Anshe Lubz, Aliyah Ledger, Rosh Hashanah, 1891, Collection of the Museum at Eldridge Street: $62 on December 1891; $27.50 on August 4, 1888; ESS Minutes, January 2, 1899 ("few dollars"; "answering the president"); January 29, 1899 ("disturbance").

32. Congregation Kahal Adath Jeshurun with Anshe Lubz, Aliyah Ledger, 1887–1890.

33. ESS Minutes, January 31, 1915; February 7, 1915; February 14, 1915.

34. S. H. Isaacs (1825–1917), an educator and one of the original members of Beth Hamedrash, was buried in an Eldridge Street Synagogue cemetery plot. *American Jewish Year Book* (Philadelphia: Jewish Publication Society of America, 1917–1918), p. 265.

35. Oral history interview of Gussie Dubrin; Wheatley, "Jews in New York," p. 330; ESS Minutes, 1890–1916 (outbursts).

CHAPTER SIX. PATRIARCHS AND MATRIARCHS

1. Warfield, *Ghetto Silhouettes*, pp. 81–82.
2. "Yarmulowski gebrakht tsu kvure mit groys koved," *Morgn ʒhurnal*, June 4, 1912.
3. Jacob Pfeffer, "Idishkeyt," *Morgn ʒhurnal*, September 18, 1908.
4. Loan Book, 1880–1902, Congregation, AJHS, RG I-10, Box 3, 1889–1902.
5. What follows is a list of the individual men and the charities they led and supported: David Cohen: Uptown Talmud Torah, Beth Israel Hospital, Lebanon Hospital, Bronx Machzike Talmud Torah, Hebrew Teachers Institute; Isaac Gellis: trustee of Beth Israel, Mount Sinai, and Lebanon Hospitals, Montefiore Home, Home of the Daughters of Jacob, Hebrew Sheltering and Immigrant Aid Society; Nathan Hutkoff: Hebrew Sheltering and Immigrant Aid Society, Beth Israel Hospital, Bronx Machzike Talmud Torah; Sender Jarmulowsky: Yorkville Talmud Torah, Kehillah, Hebrew Sheltering and Immigrant Aid Society, Beth Israel Hospital, Lebanon Hospital, Montefiore Home, Jacob Joseph Yeshiva.
6. "Reb Sender Yarmulowski," *Tageblat*, June 2, 1912.
7. "Yarmulowski in eybige ruh," *Tageblat*, June 3, 1912.
8. "Reb Sender Yarmulowski" *Tageblat*, June 2, 1912.
9. Tzedakeh Ledger, 1888–1909, Congregation, AJHS, RG I-10, Box 3.
10. "Obituary: Isaac Gellis," *Hebrew Standard*, March 30, 1906; see also "Gellis Is Dead," *Morgn ʒhurnal*, March 20, 1906; Advertisement, *Forverts*, July 7, 1933.
11. *Hebrew Standard*, March 20, 1906; see also "Izek Gellis geshtarben," *Tageblat*, March 20, 1906.
12. ESS Minutes, March 25, 1894 ("undertakes to pay"); April 24, 1894 (offered another $1,000); April 21, 1895 ("brothers").
13. ESS Minutes, January 22, 1896. The trip was planned for February 16, 1896.
14. ESS Minutes, November 7, 1897.
15. ESS Minutes, December 19, 1900; January 21, March 3, and December 10, 1901; May 29, August 17, and December 21, 1902; February 1 and February 15, 1903; January 17 and May 8, 1904; October 8, 1906.
16. "Reb Dovid Cohen," *Morgn ʒhurnal*, April 11, 1912; Special Events Ledger, February 1888, Congregation, AJHS, RG I-10, Box 17, p. 6.

17. Glenn, *Daughters of the Shtetl*, pp. 9–11; Heinze, *Adapting to Abundance*, pp. 106–107; Hyman, *Gender and Assimilation*, p. 26 (quotation); "A fleysige klal-tuer," *Morgn zhurnal*, April 21, 1911 ("such active workers").

18. "Di fershuldigte shulen," *Morgn zhurnal*, June 16, 1907 (quotations). For the percentages see Rischin, *Promised City*, p. 93. See also "East Side Losing Population," *New York Daily Tribune*, September 5, 1899.

19. ESS Minutes, May 3, 1903.

20. ESS Minutes, April 21, October 13, and November 15, 1908.

21. ESS Minutes, October 13, 1908; January 31, 1909; March 1, 1909.

22. ESS Minutes, July 22, 1909.

23. ESS Minutes, August 8, 1909; April 30, 1911.

24. "David Cohen et al. against Congregation Kahal Adath Yeshurun, Cong. Aron David and Harris Nathan of the People of the Town of Lubtz, etc.," New York Supreme Court Case, Index #8853, Part I, filed March 5, 1910, p. 5. My thanks to Jeffrey Gurock for bringing this document to my attention.

25. "Lubtzer Jews Remain with the Eldridge Street Synagogue," *Forverts*, April 14, 1911.

26. ESS Minutes, April 23, 1911.

27. "Nathan Hutkoff," *Morgn Zhurnal*, November 21, 1917.

28. "Orthodox Jews Meet," *New York Times*, December 31, 1900; "Beth Israel Hospital: A Worthy Philanthropic Institution of the East Side," *New York Times*, October 6, 1895.

29. ESS Minutes, April 10, 1898; February 3, 1902.

30. "Reb Sender Yarmulowski un zeyn tseyt," *Tageblat*, June 3, 1912.

31. Hyman, *Gender and Assimilation*, p. 97.

32. Oral history interview of Abraham Gellis, conducted by Roberta Brandes Gratz, 1991, Collection of the Museum at Eldridge Street; ESS Minutes, April 27, 1891.

33. Oral history interview of Gussie Dubrin, conducted by Judy Tenney, 1991, Collection of the Museum at Eldridge Street ("My mother"); Joseph Benjamin, "The Comforts and Discomforts of East Side Tenements," in *Report of the Year's Work* (New York: University Settlement Society, 1897), p. 27 ("Great preparations"); Edward Steiner, "The Russian and Polish Jew in New York," *Outlook*, November 1, 1902 ("Ghetto").

34. Richard Wheatley, "The Jews in New York," *Century Magazine*, January 1892, p. 327; Bertram Reinitz, "The East Side Looks into Its Future," *New York Times*, March 13, 1932.

35. "The Ghetto Market, Hester Street," *New York Times*, November 14, 1897, quoted in Schoener, *Portal to America*, p. 55; "Friday Is Market Day: Hester Street's Crowds

on the Eve of Sabbath," *New York Daily Tribune*, November 3, 1895. See also Francis McLean, "Food Stores and Purchases in the Tenth Ward," in *Report of the Year's Work* (New York: University Settlement Society, 1899), p. 15: "The market is in full swing every day and positively jams the street on Thursdays and Fridays, the days previous to the Jewish Sabbath."

36. ESS Minutes, July 19, 1903, and January 5, 1913.

37. ESS Minutes, February 3 and April 2, 1907; "David Cohen et al. against Congregation Kahal Adath Yeshurun, Cong. Aron David and Harris Nathan of the People of the Town of Lubtz, etc.," New York Supreme Court Case, Index #8853, Part I, filed March 5, 1910.

38. On women's dues see ESS Minutes, January 27, 1918; May 11, 1919; February 27, 1921. On men's dues see ESS Minutes, October 3, 1917: $5, $25; October 21, 1917: $20. On widow's dues see ESS Minutes, April 14, 1918.

39. "An East Side Charity," *New York Times*, June 23, 1895; *Morgn zhurnal*, December 29, 1926.

40. ESS Minutes, February 16, 1919.

41. Oral history interview of Naomi Groob Fuchs, conducted by Ruth Abram and Joan Bieter, June 16, 1986, Collection of the Museum at Eldridge Street.

42. Ladies' Auxiliary poster, March 20, 1935, Collection of the Museum at Eldridge Street. See also Poster announcing special meeting for a Hanukah party, December 16, 1931, Congregation, AJHS, RG I-10, Box 2.

43. Christopher Gray, "The Unmaking of a Landmark," *New York Times*, May 26, 1991. The bank runs occurred in 1917, when immigrants sought to send money to European relatives caught in World War I; the bank, run by Harry and Louis Jarmulowsky, had liabilities of $1.25 million and assets of $600,000. In August 1914, Meyer Jarmulowsky's bank at 165 East Broadway had also closed.

CHAPTER SEVEN. THE BURNING OF THE MORTGAGE

1. Wolfe, *Synagogues of the Lower East Side*, p. 35 ("prominent"); Letter from President David Parnes, January 26, 1930, Congregation, AJHS, RG I-10, Box 2 ("same position").

2. For a vivid description of changes under way on the Lower East Side, see Bertram Reinitz, "The East Side Looks into its Future, *New York Times*, March 13, 1932.

3. Ibid.

4. Oral history interview of Edwin Margolius, conducted by Renee Newman, 1996; and of Max Smith, conducted by Renee Newman, 1996, both in the Collection of the Museum at Eldridge Street.

5. "Announcement to All Brothers of Congregational Kahal Adath Jeshurun and Anshe Lubz," from David Parnes and Rafael Goldshmit [1930s], and "Special Meeting Notice," from David Parnes and Rafael Goldshmit, January 1930, both in Congregation, AJHS, RG I-10, Box 2.

6. Invitation to party, Sunday, May 8, 1932, Congregation, AJHS, RG I-10, Box 2.

7. Oral history interview of Edwin Margolius; of Naomi Groob Fuchs, conducted by Ruth Abram and Joan Bieter, 1986; of Gussie Dubrin, conducted by Judy Tenney, 1991; and of Max Smith, conducted by Renee Newman, 1996, all in the Collection of the Museum at Eldridge Street.

8. Congregation Kahal Adath Jeshurun with Anshe Lubz, *50th Anniversary Souvenir Journal*, 1934, Collection of the Museum at Eldridge Street.

9. "Help! Help!" (circular), The Relief Committee of the Lubtzer War Victims, December 1915, Collection of the Museum at Eldridge Street.

10. Fried, *Ohel Yosef*. In the preface, Fried expressed his gratitude to "all the honored leaders and members of Kahal Adath Jeshurun" for welcoming him upon his arrival in America a decade earlier and offering him a space to establish his school. The distinction between functions and roles of rabbi and preacher may have stemmed from the congregation's support of the consortium that hired Jacob Joseph as a communal rabbi, for membership in the association explicitly forbade constituent congregations from promoting their own rabbis. This allowed only for the hiring of such religious functionaries as cantor and preacher. "Constitution of the Association of the American Hebrew Orthodox Congregations," printed as appendix IV in Karp, "New York Chooses a Chief Rabbi," p. 196. The constitution states that congregations "shall not recognize any person as rabbi, but only as preacher, or Maggid, and shall not elect or appoint a *moreh hora'ah* without authority from the Chief Rabbi."

11. ESS Minutes, February 2, 1905; April 12, 1906; December 20, 1906.

12. ESS Minutes, October 27, 1918; Interview with Judge Paul P. E. Bookson, 1987, The New York Public Library–American Jewish Committee Oral History Collection, Dorot Jewish Division, The New York Public Library, Astor, Lenox and Tilden Foundations.

13. "Harav A. A. Yudelovitz, barimter gaon, toyt," *Morgn zhurnal-tageblat*, February 3, 1930 (all quotations except the last); Oral history interview of Gussie Dubrin ("He spoke"); see also "Toyzender iden fargisen trehren bay der levaye fun harav Yudelovitz," *Morgn zhurnal-tageblat*, February 4, 1930.

14. "There are several members, and householders who are not members, who will give donations [to support Yudelovitch's salary]." ESS Minutes, November 3, 1918. On congregations attending Yudelovitch's sermons, see ESS Minutes, May 11, 1919.

15. "Ale iden fun nyu-york protestiren gegen di pogromen," *Morgn zhurnal*, May 19, 1919 (closed businesses); ESS Minutes, May 18, 1919 ("shot"); Advertisement, *Morgn zhurnal*, May 19, 1919.

16. "Harav Idelson fun der eldridge strit shul is nifter gevoren," *Morgn zhurnal-tageblat*, January 17, 1943 ("greatest"; "He knew"); "Mizrakhi troyert oyf ptire fun harav Idelson," *Morgn zhurnal-tageblat*, January 17, 1943 ("first rabbis"); ESS Minutes, November 30, 1930 (contract). Idelson was a founder of Agudat Ha-Rabanim and also held high posts in Vaad Ha-Rabanim. "Harav Idelson fun der Eldridge Street Shul is nifter goveren."

17. "Toyzende menshen bay der levaye fun Mendel beyles," *Morgn zhurnal-tageblat*, July 10, 1934.

18. "Beiliss Funeral Attended by 4000," *New York Times*, July 10, 1934. For a historical account of the Beilis trial, see Lindemann, *Jew Accused*.

19. "Mendel Beilis" (editorial), *Der Tog*, July 10, 1934; Richard Wheatley, "The Jews in New York," *Century Magazine*, January 1892, p. 324; "Levaye fun Mendel Beilis" *Der Tog*, July 9, 1934.

20. "Toyzende menshen bay der levaye fun Mendel beyles," *Morgn zhurnal-tageblat*, July 10, 1934.

21. "Er iz gebliben a martirer," *Morgn zhurnal-tageblat*, July 10, 1934; Goren, *Politics and Public Culture of American Jews*, pp. 49, 82; "Levaye fun Mendel Beilis," *Der Tog* ("great impression").

22. Oral history interview of Rose Leibow Eisenberg, conducted by Roberta Brandes Gratz, 1991, Collection of the Museum at Eldridge Street; Oral history interview of Max Smith.

23. Oral history interview of Gilbert Lazarus, conducted by Roberta Brandes Gratz, 1991, Collection of the Museum at Eldridge Street.

24. Oral history interview of Naomi Groob Fuchs.

25. Oral history interview of Judge Paul P. E. Bookson, conducted by Beth Edberg, 1991, Collection of the Museum at Eldridge Street.

26. Ibid.; Oral history interview of Benjamin Markowitz, conducted by Zeke Berman, 1979, Collection of the Museum at Eldridge Street.

Selected Bibliography

COLLECTIONS OF THE MUSEUM AT ELDRIDGE STREET, NEW YORK, NY

Congregation Beth Hamedrash. Contract for Sale of Seats. 1887.

Congregation Kahal Adath Jeshurun with Anshe Lubz. Constitution. June 22, 1913.

Congregation Kahal Adath Jeshurun with Anshe Lubz. *50th Anniversary Souvenir Journal*. 1934.

Congregation Kahal Adath Jeshurun with Anshe Lubz. Ledgers and Account Books.

Congregation Kahal Adath Jeshurun with Anshe Lubz. Minute Books, 1882–1955.

Minutes of the Eldridge Street Synagogue (1890–1916). Translated by Fruma Mohrer.

Minutes of the Eldridge Street Synagogue (Selections, 1918–1944). Translated by Daniel Soyer.

Oral history interviews: Miriam Aaron, Judge Paul P. E. Bookson, Gussie Dubrin, Rose Eisenberg, Lillian Rabinowitz Fried, Naomi Groob Fuchs, Abraham Gellis, Gilbert Lazarus, Edwin Margolius, Benjamin Markowitz, Yossi Paston, Max Smith.

BOOKS AND ARTICLES

Anbinder, Tyler. *Five Points*. New York: Free Press, 2001.

Bernheimer, Charles, ed. *The Russian Jew in the United States*. Philadelphia: John C. Winston, 1905.

Diner, Hasia. *Lower East Side Memories: A Jewish Place in America*. Princeton, NJ: Princeton University Press, 2000.

———. *A Time for Gathering: The Second Migration*. Baltimore: Johns Hopkins University Press, 1995.

Diner, Hasia, Jeffrey Shandler, and Beth Wenger, eds. *Remembering the Lower East Side*. Bloomington: Indiana University Press, 2000.

Dolkart, Andrew. *Biography of a Tenement House: An Architectural History of 97 Orchard Street*. Santa Fe: Center for American Places, 2006.

Eisenstein, Judah D. *Ozar Zikhronothai: Autobiography and Memoirs* [in Hebrew]. New York: J. D. Eisenstein, 1929.

———. "The History of the First Russian-American Jewish Congregation: The Beth Hamedrash Hagadol." *Publications of the American Jewish Historical Society* 9 (1901): 63–74.

Fried, Yosef Eliyahu. *Ohel Yosef*. New York: Rosenberg, 1903.

Glenn, Susan. *Daughters of the Shtetl*. Ithaca, NY: Cornell University Press, 1990.

Glogower, Rod. "Responsa Literature," *American Jewish History* (December, 1979).

Goldman, Karla. *Beyond the Synagogue Gallery*. Cambridge: Harvard University Press, 2000.

Goren, Arthur A. *New York Jews and the Quest for Community: The Kehillah Experiment, 1908–1922*. New York: Columbia University Press, 1970.

———. *The Politics and Public Culture of American Jews*. Bloomington: University of Indiana Press, 1999.

———. "Public Ceremonies Defining Central Synagogue." In Elizabeth Blackmar and Arthur A. Goren, eds., *Congregating and Consecrating at Central Synagogue*. New York: Central Synagogue, 2003.

Grinstein, Hyman. *The Rise of the Jewish Community of New York, 1654–1860*. Philadelphia: Jewish Publication Society, 1945.

Gurock, Jeffrey. *American Jewish Orthodoxy in Historical Perspective*. Hoboken, NJ: Ktav, 1996.

———. "The Orthodox Synagogue." In Wertheimer, *American Synagogue*.

———. "A Stage in the Emergence of the Americanized Synagogue among East European Jews." *Journal of American Ethnic History* (Spring 1990): 7–25.

————. "Synagogue Imperialism in New York City: The Case of Congregation Kehal Adath Jeshurun, 1909–1911." *Michael* 15 (2000): 95–108.

Hall, David, ed. *Lived Religion in America: Toward a History of Practice.* Princeton, NJ: Princeton University Press, 1997.

Hapgood, Hutchins. *The Spirit of the Ghetto.* New York, 1902.

Heinze, Andrew. *Adapting to Abundance: Jewish Immigrants, Mass Consumption, and the Search for American Identity.* New York: Columbia University Press, 1990.

Hertzberg, Arthur. "Treifene Medina: Learned Opposition to Emigration to the United States." *Proceedings of the Eighth World Congress of Jewish Studies, 1981: Panel Sessions, Jewish History.* Jerusalem: World Union of Jewish Studies, 1981.

Holscher, Lucian. "Secularization and Urbanization in the Nineteenth Century: An Interpretive Model." In Hugh McLeod, ed., *European Religion in the Age of the Great Cities.* London: Routledge, 1995.

Howe, Irving. *The World of Our Fathers.* New York: Harcourt, Brace, 1976.

Hunnicut, Benjamin. "Jewish Sabbath Movement in the Early 20th Century." *American Jewish History* 79 (December 1979): 196–225.

Hyman, Paula. *Gender and Assimilation in Modern Jewish History: The Roles and Representation of Women.* Seattle: University of Washington Press, 1995.

————. "Immigrant Women and Consumer Protest: The New York City Kosher Meat Boycott of 1902." *American Jewish History* 70 (1980): 91–105.

Jewish Communal Register of New York City, 1917–1918. New York: Kehillah Jewish Community, 1918.

Jick, Leon A. *The Americanization of the Synagogue, 1820–1870.* Hanover, NH: Published for Brandeis University Press by the University Press of New England, 1976.

Joselit, Jenna W. *New York's Jewish Jews: The Orthodox Community in the Interwar Years.* Bloomington: Indiana University Press, 1990.

————. *The Wonders of America: Reinventing Jewish Culture.* New York: Hill and Wang, 1994.

Joseph, Samuel. *Jewish Immigration to the United States, 1881–1910.* New York: Columbia University Press, 1914.

Kahan, Arcadius, "Economic Problems and Some Pilgrims' Progress: Jewish Immigration from Eastern Europe in the U.S., 1890–1914." *Journal of Economic History* 38, no. 1 (1978): 101–127.

Kamil, Seth, and Eric Wakin, eds. *The Big Onion Guide to New York City.* New York: New York University Press, 2002.

Kaplan, Marion A. *The Making of the Jewish Middle Class: Women, Family and Identity in Imperial Germany.* New York: Oxford University Press, 1991.

Karp, Abraham. "New York Chooses a Chief Rabbi." *Publications of the American Historical Society* 44 (1955): 129–198.

Kaufman, David. *Shul with a Pool: The Synagogue Center in American Jewish History.* Hanover, NH: University Press of New England, 1999.

Kessner, Thomas. *The Golden Door: Italian and Jewish Immigrants in New York City, 1880–1915.* New York: Oxford University Press, 1977.

Krinsky, Carol. *Synagogues of Europe: Architecture, History, Meaning.* Cambridge: MIT Press, 1985.

Kuznets, Simon. "Immigration of Russian Jews to the United States: Background and Structure," *Perspectives in American History* 9 (1975): 35–124.

Liebman, Charles S. *The Ambivalent American Jew: Politics, Religion and Family in American Jewish Life.* Philadelphia: Jewish Publication Society of America, 1973.

Lindemann, Albert. *The Jew Accused: Three Anti-Semitic Affairs (Dreyfus, Beilis, Frank), 1894–1915.* New York: Cambridge University Press, 1991.

Marcus, Jacob. *Concise Dictionary of American Jewish Biography.* Brooklyn: Carson Publishing, 1994.

McLeod, Hugh, ed. *European Religion in the Age of Great Cities, 1830–1930.* London: Routledge, 1995.

Mendelsohn, Joyce. *The Lower East Side Remembered and Revisited.* New York: Lower East Side Press, 2001.

Michels, Tony. *A Fire in Their Hearts: Yiddish Socialists in New York.* Cambridge: Harvard University Press, 2005.

Orsi, Robert Anthony. *The Madonna of 115th Street: Faith and Community in Italian Harlem, 1880–1950.* New Haven: Yale University Press, 1985.

Park, Robert E., and Herbert A. Miller. *Old World Traits Transplanted*. New York: Harper and Brothers, 1921.

Prell, Riv-Ellen. *Community and Prayer: The Havurah in American Judaism*. Detroit. MI: Wayne State University Press, 1989.

Price, George M. "The Russian Jews in America." *Publications of the American Jewish Historical Society* (September, December 1958). Originally published as *Russkie Yevrei v Amerike* (Saint Petersburg, 1893).

Raphael, Marc Lee. "The Origins of Organized National Jewish Philanthropy in the United States, 1914–1939." In Rischin, *Jews of North America*.

Rischin, Moses, ed. *The Jews of North America*. Detroit, MI: Wayne State University Press, 1987.

———. *The Promised City: New York's Jews, 1870–1914*. Cambridge: Harvard University Press, 1962.

Rothkoff, Aaron. "The American Sojourns of Ridbaz: The Religious Problems within the Immigrant Community." *American Jewish Historical Quarterly* 57 (June 1968): 557–572.

Sanders, Ronald. *The Downtown Jews*. New York: Dover, 1969.

Sarna, Jonathan. *American Judaism*. New Haven: Yale University Press, 2004.

Schoener, Allon, ed. *Portal to America: The Lower East Side, 1870–1925*. New York: Holt, Rinehart and Winston, 1967.

Slobin, Mark, *Chosen Voices: The Story of the American Cantorate*. Chicago: University of Illinois Press, 1989

———. *Tenement Songs: The Popular Music of the Jewish Immigrants*. Chicago: University of Illinois Press, 1982.

Soltes, Mordecai. *The Yiddish Press: An Americanizing Agency*. New York: Columbia University, 1925.

Soyer, Daniel. *Jewish Immigrant Associations and American Identity in New York, 1880–1939*. Cambridge: Harvard University Press, 1997.

Stanislawski, Michael. "Russian Jewry, the Russian State, and the Dynamics of Jewish Emancipation." In Pierre Birnbaum and Ira Katznelson, eds., *Paths of Emancipation: Jews, States and Citizenship*. Princeton, NJ: Princeton University Press, 1995.

Steffens, Lincoln. *The Autobiography of Lincoln Steffens*. New York: Harcourt, Brace, 1931.

Stewart, John Donald. "A Programme for the Preservation of Synagogue Kahal Adath Jeshurun with Anshe Lubz." Master's thesis, Columbia University, 1979.

Warfield, David. *Ghetto Silhouettes*. New York: James Pott, 1902.

Weinberger, Moses. *People Walk on Their Heads: Jews and Judaism in New York*. Translated and edited by Jonathan D. Sarna. New York: Holmes and Meier, 1982.

Wenger, Beth S. *New York Jews and the Great Depression: Uncertain Promise*. New Haven: Yale University Press, 1996.

Wertheimer, Jack, ed. *The American Synagogue: A Sanctuary Transformed*. Cambridge: Cambridge University Press, 1987.

————, ed. *Jewish Religious Leadership: Image and Reality*. New York: Jewish Theological Press, 2004.

Wiernik, Peter. *History of the Jews in America*. New York: Jewish Press, 1912.

Williams, Sarah. "Urban Popular Religion and Rites of Passage." In Hugh McLeod, *European Religion in the Age of Great Cities, 1830–1930*. London: Routledge, 1995.

Wischnitzer, Rachel. *Synagogue Architecture in the United States: History and Interpretation*. Philadelphia: Jewish Publication Society of America, 1955.

Wolfe, Gerard. *The Synagogues of New York's Lower East Side*. New York: Washington Mews / New York University Press, 1978.

Yezierska, Anzia. *Hungry Hearts*. Cambridge, MA: Riverside Press, 1920.

Zaludkowski, Elisa. *Kultur-treger fun der idisher liturgye*. Detroit, MI: Zaludkowski, 1930.

Zipperstein, Steven. *The Jews of Odessa: A Cultural History, 1794–1881*. Stanford, CA: Stanford University Press, 1985.

Index

ESS is an abbreviation for "Eldridge Street Synagogue." Locators in italics indicate illustrations.

Aaron, Miriam, 77–78, 79

Abrahams, Isidor, 35, 70

Adler, Felix, Dr., 12

Agudes ha-Kehillos. *See* Association of American Hebrew Orthodox Congregations

Allen Street property, 7, 19, 20–21, 22, 25, 28, 29

American Hebrew (newspaper), 41, 42

American Israelite (newspaper), 36–37, 38–40, 41

Americanization of Judaism: changing roles of rabbis, 125–29; communal leadership roles, 90–91, 106; Conservative Judaism, 35, 39–40; diversity of synagogue membership, 18–19, 67–69; patriotism, *9*, 12–13, *118*; religious education of children, 37, 39–40; synagogue architecture as reflection of, 23–24, 42, 80–81; Torah reading, 81; women's balcony, 75–77. *See also* decorum; entrepreneurship; Orthodox Judaism; Reform Judaism; Sabbath observance

Anshe Bialystock, 68

Anshe Lubz, merger with ESS, 102–4, 109

Anshe Sfard synagogue, 30, 139n21

Anshe Suwalk synagogue, 51, 57, 68, 114

anti-Semitism, 127–29

architecture of ESS: American sensibility reflected in, 23–24, 40, 42; arcade, 23; ark, 3, *6*, 35, *46*, 70; balcony seating for women, 4, 75–78, *77*, *79*, 88, 106; banisters, 78, *79;* barrel-vaulted ceiling, *38; bes medresh*, 91, 92, *93*, 99, 116, 134; bimah, 64, *65*, 66, 79, 83; cantor's stand, *50;* chandeliers, *5*, *9*, *38;* construction costs, 25–26, *26;* doors, 25, 105–6, *106;* electricity, 4, 5, *5*, *6;* eternal light, 35; facade, 4, *24*, 32, *33;* finials, 34, *47*, 48; flagholders, 12–*13;* grooves in floor from *shokeling*, 67, *68;* horseshoe arches, 32; influence on Lower East Side synagogues, 47–48; Jewish numerology reflected in, 24; Matriarchs reflected in, 25, 105–6, *106;* pillars, 37; Sabbath reflected in, 45–46; spittoons, 21, 82, *83;* Stars of David, 32, *34;* stylistic influences on, 23–24, 32, 34, 47; Ten Commandments, 4, 6, 45; terra cotta, *34*, *45;* windows, 3, 16, 23–25, 32, 44–45, *45*, *115*

ark, 3, *6*, 35, *46*, 70

artist's sketch of service at ESS, 78–79, *80*

Ash, Abraham Joseph, Rabbi, 17, 18, 20, 137n4

Association of American Hebrew Orthodox Congregations, 10, 41–42, 94, 96

attendance at synagogue services, 38, 40, 73–74, 75, 144n18

windows, stained-glass, 3, 16, 23–25, 32, 44–45, *45, 115*

Wolfe, Gerard, 3, 134, 135n4

women: attendance at services, 75; attention to sermons, 78; balcony seating for, 4, 76–77, *77;* charity work of, 109–10; entrance to ESS, 75; food preparation by, 107, 111; four doors representing the Matriarchs, 25, 105–6, *106;* as *khevre kedishe* attendants, 109; kosher meat boycott (1902), 64–66; ladies' auxiliaries, 8, 106, 110–13, *113;* and *mikvahs,* 20, 27–30, *29,* 107, 139n19, 139–40n22; philanthropy of, 107, 109; Sabbath observance by, 30, 108–9; as seatholders, 27–28; synagogue membership and, 71; wealth and social status of, 109–10; widows, 109–10; wigmakers, 27, 28

women's auxiliaries, 8, 106, 110–13, *113*

World War: I, 12, 124–25; II, 134

yeshivas, 93–94, 96, 126, 127, 137n14

Yezierska, Anzia, 44

Yiddish language, 37, 42

Yiddish press: Beilis trial in, 128, 129–30; on cantors, 54, *60,* 60–61; concert advertisements, *61,* 124–25, 132, *133;* on ESS paying off the mortgage, 132; and Gellis Sausage Company, 96–97; Idelson's eulogy at Beilis's funeral, 129; on indifference to community welfare, 58; Jewish businessmen in, 91; kosher meat boycott in, 65, 66; on merger of ESS with Anshe Lubz, 103; *mikvah* advertisement in, 28; on movement of wealthy Jews from Lower East Side, 101; response to anti-Semitic riots in Europe, 127; tributes to ESS presidents, 94–95, 104–5; tribute to Sarah Gellis, 110; on uptown branch of ESS, 103

Yiddish theaters, 127

Yidishe gazeten (newspaper), 16, 28, 40–41, 49

Yidishe tageblat (newspaper), 40

Yom Kippur. *See* High Holidays

Yudelovitch, Avrohom Aharon, Rabbi, *126;* oratorical fame, 78, 118, 127; response to anti-Semitic riots in Europe, 127; scholarship of, 118, 125–26

Zichron Ephraim Synagogue, 56, 100

Zionism, 124, 127, 128